Glazes & Glazing

Finishing Techniques

Glazes & Glazing

Ceramic Arts Handbook Series

Edited by Anderson Turner

The American Ceramic Society
600 N. Cleveland Ave., Suite 210
Westerville, Ohio 43082

www.CeramicArtsDaily.org

The American Ceramic Society
600 N. Cleveland Ave., Suite 210
Westerville, OH 43082

12 11 10 09 08   5 4 3 2 1

ISBN: 978-1-57498-295-4

Every effort has been made to ensure that all the information in this book is accurate. Due to differing conditions, equipment, tools, and individual skills, the publisher cannot be responsible for any injuries, losses, and other damages that may result from the use of the information in this book. Final determination of the suitability of any information, procedure or product for use contemplated by any user, and the manner of that use, is the sole responsibility of the user. This book is intended for informational purposes only.

The views, opinions and findings contained in this book are those of the author. The publishers, editors, reviewers and author assume no responsibility or liability for errors or any consequences arising from the use of the information contained herein. Registered names and trademarks, etc., used in this publication, even without specific indication thereof, are not to be considered unprotected by the law. Mention of trade names of commercial products does not constitute endorsement or recommendation for use by the publishers, editors or authors.

Publisher: Charles Spahr, President, Ceramic Publications Company, a wholly owned subsidiary of The American Ceramic Society

Art Book Program Manager: Bill Jones

Series Editor: Anderson Turner

Graphic Design and Production: Melissa Bury, Bury Design, Westerville, Ohio

Cover Images: Vase by Jeff Kleckner; (top right) platter by Tom Coleman; (bottom right) "Pampas Vase" by Paul McCoy.

Frontispiece: "Testimonial Urn II" by Paul McCoy

Printed in China

Contents

Preface

My first experience where I wished for quality glaze results was during my junior year of high school. I was lucky enough to have a fabulous teacher, Pete Cooper, who saw the artist in me, and perhaps more importantly, he had me moving a lot of material (clay). I wedged, I rolled, I threw, I glazed—it was the first time the entire ceramic process was presented to me in such a complete way. We talked about concepts as well as the technical. It was great, and I know countless teachers like Mr. Cooper share the same type of knowledge everyday with their students.

I remember one day talking to him about ceramics over a just-fired kiln load and him saying something along the lines of "Most of these things aren't very interesting, but there are always a few gems. You can tell when someone has thought through an idea and considered what the final glazed result might look like . . . Others just pick something fun or pretty and don't care about the result." That conversation has stayed with me over the years, and it's within that context that I've selected the content for this book.

We have so many options in glazing today, even though the mystery of what happens in the kiln has long since gone by the wayside with our ability to more easily control our firings. And we're able to learn through a wealth of shared information on how to change the surface of any ceramic work to denote whatever type of intrigue we deem fit. It's ceramics by any means and no glaze or surface treatment is off limits.

But what Mr. Cooper shared with me still holds true, although I would add that what we do to the surface of our work is often as important as the form itself. Too often an artist makes a poor glaze choice when a quality choice was within their reach.

This book contains information on all aspects of glazing from the simple to the complex and highly technical. And here too are the stories and experiences of several artists that I hope will inspire you in much the way Pete Cooper inspired me.

We who love clay are lucky. This is a medium that never ceases to challenge or surprise. I hope you're able to find some surprises in what others have presented here.

Anderson Turner

Using Gravity to Enhance a Glaze Surface

by Kari E. Radasch

Large serving platter, 20 inches in length, terra cotta with White Slip and Kari's Best Transparent Glaze.

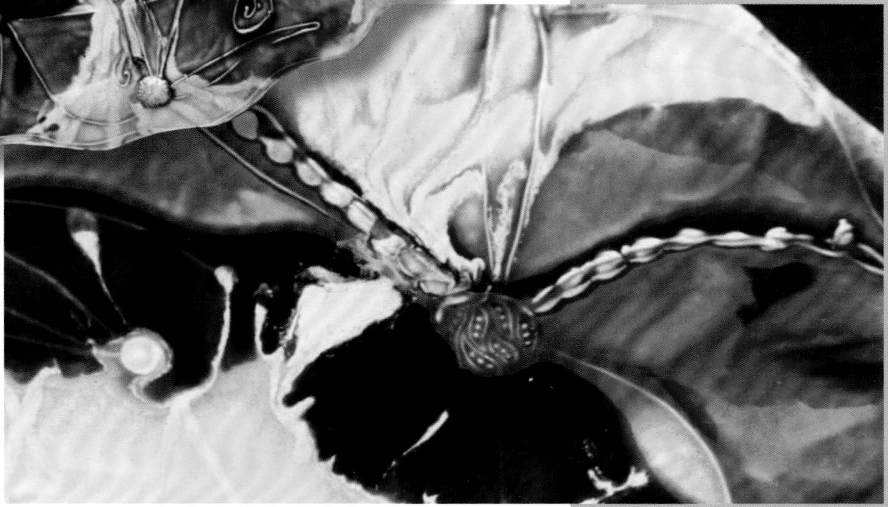

Detail of large serving platter, shown above.

I t is a shallow notion to insist that low-fire work lacks the glaze depth that stoneware and porcelains claim to have. On the contrary, it is as much the case that high-fire work lacks the glaze depth of terra cotta. There are many reasons for this misperception, but the most preeminent one, in my opinion, is that our low-fire vocabulary is not as developed as our high-fire one. We will begin to fix that right here.

Surface is more than a seductive veneer; at its best it engages the clay. My surfaces begin from the minute I touch the clay, with the rolling out of coils, the pounding out of slabs and the pinching of forms. I embrace spontaneous yet purposeful marks—brush trails, glaze drips and thinly applied slips. I try to embed as much information as possible in the making so that the glaze can respond accordingly. These marks have a huge impact on the finished glaze surface. They aid in building layers and provide a variety of terrain and textures to which the glazes respond. These marks are not only functional, but they tell a story. They recall motions and actions of the maker. This veneer adds another layer of surface and meaning.

1

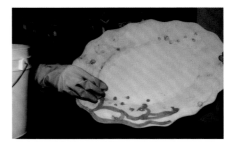

After using a pencil to divide and mark the areas for the different glazes, I brush the bisqueware with a copper carbonate wash over all of the slip-trailed and textured surfaces. I wipe the copper carbonate off, allowing it to be trapped in the piped slip and sprigged buttons. Since it is a strong flux, it increases the melt, encouraging the glazes to run and pool over these slip barriers.

CAUTION

Limited exposure to copper is considered relatively safe; however, copper carbonate is a heavy metal, so to be safe, I always wear latex gloves when wiping off the copper wash.

Glazes that run the most are brushed on, then stiffer glazes are piped out of a syringe. For example, two transparent gloss glazes—tinted to have amber and pink tones—are brushed into the demarcated pencil areas. Then pink majolica is applied (using a syringe) on top.

Finally, for added insurance, I will encourage specific areas of glaze to melt by adding copper carbonate wash on top of the glaze. This combination of stiff and fluid glazes, along with gravity, provided the effects I desire.

I work with a terra cotta to which I add 2–4% red iron oxide and burnt umber. I do this for two reasons: to encourage an active interface between the clay and glaze, and to make the clay rich and chocolaty. I use terra-cotta clay because of its robust nature, its visual weight, the way it records a surface and the way it responds to my touch. I begin by making marks such as fingerprints, incisions, tracings, inscriptions and serrations from a rib. Next, I may emboss areas of the slab with architectural motifs reminiscent of decorative tile and tin ceiling panels. I then place a heavy white slip over the entire piece using a large mop brush, topping it off with a much thicker slip piped through a syringe. The final wet step is attaching candy-like buttons made from a thickened version of the white slip. One of my first important realizations was that I needed to use glazes with different melting points. Their differing viscosities gives them dimension and prevents them from looking too shiny or flat. After hundreds of glaze tests using several standard glazes (transparent gloss, satin white opaque and majolica), I began layering and floating glazes upon one another. I ended up choosing a majolica because of its thick, stiff marshmallowy looking qualities, and two different transparent gloss glazes (one that is accepting of stains and another that is a barium-fritted glaze, reminiscent of those luscious lead glazes).

I also started paying close attention to gravity, watching how glazes move, melt and flow depending upon their mass, temperature and location on the pot. I have found two things that help my glazes flow better during application: I add both CMC Gum (0.6%) for brushability and Veegum T (1.6–1.8%, depending on how heavily the glaze is fritted) for suspension. I also have found that spraying each pot with a mist of water (aside from washing the bisque before glazing) not only lessens the pinholes but acts as a provisional vehicle that assists in achieving an even, flowing first glaze coat.

I have no doubt that the most consistent method of firing is to use pyrometric cones. I have learned this through experience. Firing with cones ensures that your results will be as true as possible. However, some of my more important aesthetic decisions have been based on firing mistakes. One of these mistakes led to my decision to fire to a soft cone 02.

Dinner plate, 10 inches in diameter, terra cotta with White Slip and Kari's Best Transparent Glaze.

Raising my firing temperature is the final step in encouraging my glazes to move more than they would at cone 04. The added benefits are a stronger clay and glaze interface, and a more vitreous clay body.

NOTE

CMC is an organic gum and will break down over time (not only will it stop working, but it has the potential to develop an odor). When left to dry, CMC creates a hard glaze coat, which is great if it is necessary to transport your wares, but when left in a brush, the gum will act like a glue—sticking the bristles together, making it tough to wash out.

Recipes

White Slip
Cone 04–02

Talc	40.0 %
Nepheline Syenite	10.0
Ball Clay	40.0
Silica	10.0
	100.0 %
Add: Zircopax	7.0 %

Kari's Best Transparent Glaze
Cone 04–02

Gerstley Borate	11.0 %
Talc	30.0
Pemco Frit P-626	19.0
Ferro Frit 3124	11.0
Spodumene	14.0
EPK Kaolin	15.0
	100.0 %
Add: Wollastonite	5.0 %
Veegum T	1.0 %
CMC Gum	0.4 %

Celadon
Copper Carbonate	0.3 %

Blue
Cobalt Carbonate	1.5 %
Copper Carbonate	2.0 %

Grape
Manganese Dioxide	7.0 %
Copper Carbonate	0.5 %

Emerald Green
Copper Carbonate	6.0 %

Woody Hughes Base
Cone 04–02

Gerstley Borate	26.0 %
Lithium Carbonate	4.0
Nepheline Syenite	20.0
Ferro Frit 3124	30.0
EPK Kaolin	10.0
Silica	10.0
	100.0 %
Add: Veegum T	1.6 %
CMC Gum	0.5 %

For soft color that will remain transparent, add 7% stain.

Majolica
Cone 04–02

Ferro Frit 3124	66.3 %
Ferro Frit 3110	15.9
Ferro Frit 5301	0.5
EPK Kaolin	17.3
	100.0 %
Add: Zircopax	15.9 %
Veegum T	1.6 %
CMC Gum	0.5 %

For soft color, add 7% stain.

Todd Burns
Transfering Imagery

by Karen C. Britt

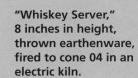

**"Whiskey Server,"
8 inches in height,
thrown earthenware,
fired to cone 04 in an
electric kiln.**

After spending time with Todd Burns, it comes as no surprise to learn that he initially studied philosophy in college before deciding to change his major to Fine Arts in order to pursue ceramics. His work reveals that he didn't leave philosophical interests entirely behind; what philosophers work out in words, Burns gives visual representation in ceramics. In his current body of work, one has only to think of the connection with Aristotle and his school of Peripatetics' interest in biological research. With its intensive work on the description and classification of plants, and its investigations into the physiology of plant life, the Peripatetics strengthened the bond between philosophy and what would today be considered science. Although more than 2000 years separate Burns from the Greek philosophers, they are evoked by the persistent juxtaposition of past and present, literal and metaphorical in his work.

On his vessels, Burns has turned his attention to an exploration of marine iconography. It is immediately obvious that his aim is neither to produce the generic fish and nautical motifs of tourist wares nor to create iconography, which is inextricably linked to the shape of the vessel such as the Marine Style pottery of the Bronze Age Aegean. His approach to the surface is vastly different—a difference that is best explained by the disjuncture of time and space. Burns turns decidedly to the historical past for the shapes of his forms and iconography. At first glance, form and subject appear incongruous, and yet they are threads of a single tapestry in which the historical as well as the artist's personal past are interwoven. The shapes of the vessels range from teapots and ewers to jars and vases. For some of the forms, the source of inspiration was the late fifteenth and sixteenth century majolica pharmacological vessels produced in Tuscany and Emilia. These highly decorated jars were made to store herbs and other substances used for medicinal purposes by some of the wealthiest families in northern Italy. The jars were decorated with heavily stylized foliate scrolls, family crests and other insignia. Against the background of floral motifs, a single unfurled scroll contained the label, carefully written in 'Gothic script,' which identified the contents of the jar.

As a child growing up in Kansas, Burns was fascinated by wildlife and the natural environment. His interest in complex biological and chemical processes led him to spend long periods of time in a field near his rural home. He requested a chemistry set for his fourteenth birthday which only increased his appreciation for the scientific orderliness of the natural world. His high school art teacher encouraged his self-exploration and curiosity by sending him home with a pottery wheel for the summer. For Burns, ceramics provided an escape from difficult teenage years. Yet, he never thought of ceramics as more than a hobby so, when he enrolled at Wichita State University, it did not occur to him to consider majoring in Fine Arts. Enrolling in a ceramics class not only prompted Burns to change his major, but also the course of his life.

For financial reasons, Burns was forced to leave school after one year to seek full-time employment. While he worked in construction during the day, Burns cleaned the studio at a community art center at night in exchange for studio time. During this period, he developed a portfolio of work. A serendipitous meeting with visiting artist John Neely,

professor of ceramics at Utah State University, provided the opening Burns had been waiting for. A full scholarship to Utah State altered his career trajectory in a manner he had never anticipated. In Utah, he experienced a rare confluence of circumstances: in his mentor, Burns found someone who was methodical and had a deep appreciation for detail in his own work. Further, he transformed a long-standing interest in nature into a true passion for the outdoors, particularly fly-fishing.

His lifelong interest in scientific methodology and the deconstruction of complex processes are recurring themes in Burns' work. However, in the Marine vessels he combines these with his passion for fly-fishing and respect for intricate detail. The choice of Italian Renaissance pharmacological shapes for his vessels expresses postmodern society's need for historical roots, but also appeals to Burns' appreciation for the rigors of scientific methodology: the careful arrangement of substances into clearly labeled containers. The exuberance of the floral motifs on his vessels is tempered by the detail and precision of the fish, scrolls and carefully rendered knots. His source for the marine iconography is McClane's Standard Fishing Encyclopedia and International Angling Guide, a typically mid-twentieth century encyclopedia, which includes exhaustive descriptions and detailed illustrations of fish and the instruments used in fishing. The loss of continuity in pottery workshop traditions in the

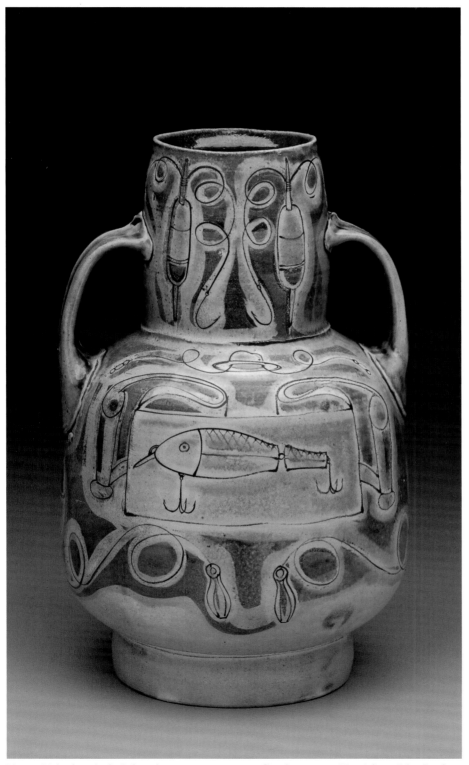

Vase, 14 inches in height, thrown stoneware, fired to cone 10 with residual salt.

Tools for Transferring Imagery

In the studio, Burns is surrounded by an incongruous assortment of tools: a digital camera, laptop and printer on the one hand, and a banding wheel, pot and brushes on the other. He uses modern technology creatively as a vehicle to the past. He photographs the marine imagery, which will be placed inside the large scrolls on the sides of the vessels. Next, he maps out and measures the space of the scroll. Using Photoshop, he changes the size of the image to correspond with that of the scroll. After printing the image, Burns transfers it onto the pot using homemade carbon paper which he developed to perfect the transfer process. With black underglaze stain and a pen liner brush, he meticulously goes over the faint pencil and carbon lines. Next, he loosely brushes latex wax resist over all of the lines and selected areas to prevent underglaze attachment. Finally, using a soft brush, he applies a diluted version of the black underglaze to the entire surface, which provides depth to his compositions while simultaneously preventing the figures from disappearing into the background.

Teapot, 7 inches in height, thrown earthenware, fired to cone 04 in an electric kiln.

modern era has led to an inability to interpret the original meaning and symbolism layered in these works. Burns responded to this void by creating a visual language that is simultaneously historical and personal.

Process

The decoration of the surface of a vessel generally takes one day. The surface treatment of his wheel-thrown pots has an imperfect quality: rims are uneven and the handles are roughly attached to the body of the vessel. Once the form is finished, Burns puts the vessel on a banding wheel. He decides on the size and placement of the most prominent motif, the scroll. As he spins the pot, Burns uses a pencil to mark the top and bottom of the scroll. Next he draws the scroll, leaving the inside blank. At this stage, he draws by free-hand the foliate design that serves as the background and unites both sides of the vessel. In many cases, the floral imagery has been replaced with fishing line and fishing implements arranged to form foliate spirals. At first glance, they appear to be stylized floral motifs; however, when the viewer looks more closely it becomes apparent that Burns has substituted personal iconography for the formal decorative imagery. The skill with which he transforms fishing line, hooks, bobs and sinkers into lively organic spirals proves that decorative and symbolic are not mutually exclusive concepts.

At this stage, Burns turns inward, recalling memories of moments of discovery, delight and enchantment with the natural world. He often consults McClane's Encyclopedia either randomly or with a specific goal in mind. A teapot with a mouse exemplifies Burns' process. While teaching at Interlochen School for the Arts, Burns would often fish at night. He read that using a fly that looked like a mouse had been successful in luring trout. Burns tried the mouse fly and, to his astonishment, the trout went for it—missing twice—before finally being caught. This moment of discovery is captured on the teapot by the depiction of a brown trout along with the mouse fly; illustrations of both were found in McClane's Encyclopedia.

On many of Burns' vessels the glaze covers the top half of the form while the bottom half is unglazed in order to achieve an unfinished appearance similar to the Persian and majolica traditions that were inspired by Chinese porcelain. The floral motifs of the background frame the scrolls on each side. They extend over most of the available glazed space and, although arranged symmetrically to bring unity to the background, there is an inherent liveliness in the rendering. Among the motifs that appear frequently in Burns' iconographical lexicon are knots. From a literal standpoint, knots are integral to fishing; however, the broader significance of knots in Burns' work is representative of the many metaphorical allusions contained in his compositions. From the recognition of their protective qualities in the

Vase, 13 inches in height, thrown stoneware, fired to cone 10 with residual salt, by Todd Burns.

Middle Ages to their contemporary associations of union, knots have long been symbolic motifs in the history of art. In work that mediates the past and present in technique, subject and the layering of meaning, Burns' aim isn't to accurately represent the natural world but rather to bring logic, order and harmony to his compositions, which, in turn, become metaphors for the basic needs and desires of humankind.

Recipes

Amber Celadon
Cone 10

Gerstley Borate	4.3 %
Whiting	11.4
Wollastonite	20.0
Custer Feldspar	31.4
Albany Slip	8.6
EPK Kaolin	4.3
Silica	20.0
	100.0 %
Add: Yellow Ochre	12.9 %

Andy Martin Chartreuse
Cone 10

Barium Carbonate	6.7 %
Lithium Carbonate	4.5
Ferro Frit 3110	44.9
Tile #6	13.4
Silica	30.5
	100.0 %
Add: Bentonite	3.1 %
Chrome	0.5 %

Burns Alkali Blue
Cone 10

Barium	6.0 %
Ferro Frit 3110	38.0
Spodumene	19.0
EPK Kaolin	12.0
Silica	25.0
	100.0 %
Add: Copper Carbonate	2–5.0 %
Bentonite	3.0 %

Pete's Best Clear
Cone 03-04

Gerstley Borate	35.0%
Pemco Frit P-626	25.0
Spodumene	20.0
Kaolin	20.0
	100.0 %

Apple Green Variation

Copper Carbonate	2.0%
Red Iron Oxide	1.0%

Yellow Variation

Red Iron Oxide	2.0 %

Simple Gloss
Cone 04

Gerstley Borate	55.0 %
Kaolin	30.0
Silica	15.0
	100.0 %

Amber Variation

Manganese Dioxide	5–9.0 %

Green Variation

Copper Carbonate	5–9.0 %

Glazing Patterns

by Frank James Fisher

Glaze application methods are as infinite as our imagination. Nearly every item around my studio or house has the potential to be a glaze applicator. It just takes a little imagination to see the potential, and experimenting is key to discovering new ideas. For every new idea, there is a pile of attempts. But don't be too quick to discard the failures. Hidden in almost every failure are the beginnings of a new success, you just need to look at it in the right context.

Here are three glaze application techniques. Each demonstrates a different approach to evaluating and using objects to create unique glaze patterns. The first method is a direct contact approach, the second is a stenciling approach, and the third is a transfer approach. A small sponge roller is used to demonstrate these three approaches to applying glaze.

The direct approach involves dipping an object into glaze (in this case a sponge roller) and pressing the object against the surface. The shape of the object and the action used to apply the glaze determines the type of mark it leaves. The object can be soft and absorbent like a sponge roller or it can be rigid like a kitchen spatula—any object can leave a unique mark.

The stencil approach involves applying glaze through or around another object. This mark is based on a positive versus negative image. The cheese cloth acts as a stencil and the roller is the applicator. After applying the glaze through the cloth, a unique grid of squares is created. Other materials with an open weave, for example, lace curtains, can also be used.

The transfer approach involves selecting a textured object, applying glaze to its raised surface and printing the texture onto the ceramic surface. Any object that has a distinct texture can be used. The glaze is rolled onto the object. The image is transferred by pressing the glazed object against the pot's surface. Bubble wrap (used for shipping) became the transferred texture for this demonstration. The resulting star-like shapes wrap around the surface to form a unique glaze pattern.

By using everyday objects for these glazing techniques, an entire new world of glaze marks and patterns awaits discovery.

Glazing Patterns: Direct Approach

Wipe the bisque surface with a damp sponge, then pour the glaze over the surface while slowly rotating the bottle.

After coating the bottle with glaze, quickly shake the bottle downward to remove drops from the base.

After wiping the foot clean with a sponge, glaze the recessed base with a brush.

Dip the bottle top quickly into the second glaze color, overlapping the glazes.

Brush the glaze on the bare bisque of the bottle opening.

Bottle, white stoneware, fired to cone 6, glazed with Warm Jade Green and Licorice Black.

Set up the roller and pour glaze into the tray.

After absorbing glaze into the sponge roller, dab the glaze in a pattern onto the bottle.

Stencil Approach

Complete steps 1–5 on previous page. To create a stencil texture, hold a piece of cheescloth in position on the bottle.

Using a sponge roller, roll the glaze over the cheesecloth.

Peel away cheesecloth to reveal texture. Experiment with other open materials such as lace, nylon window screen, etc.

Transfer Approach

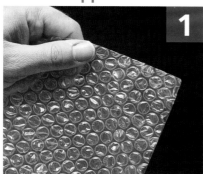

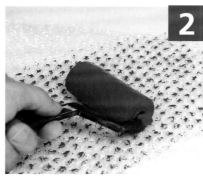

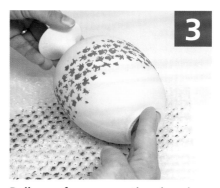

Complete steps 1 through 3 on previous page. For this method, you'll transfer a pattern, which, in this example is bubble wrap.

Roll the glaze onto the domed pills of the bubble wrap.

Roll your form across the glazed bubble wrap.

The completed glazed texture wraps around the entire form. At this point, dip the bottle top quickly into a second overlapping glaze if you want.

Bottle, white stoneware, cone 6 oxidation, glazed with Warm Jade Green and Licorice Black.

Bottle, white stoneware, cone 6 oxidation, glazed with Shelly's Blue and Licorice Black

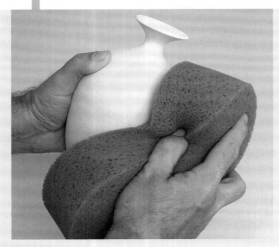

Glazing Tips

- Glaze needs a firm clean surface to cling onto, so wipe the your bisqueware before glazing. Fine dust builds up quickly in a studio, and this is true even if the pots were removed immedately from a bisque kiln. Glaze can slide off an un-wiped pot onto a kiln shelf during firing.

- Glazing very dry bisque surfaces results in an extra-thick glaze application, because the mois-ture from the wet glaze is quickly sucked into the dry bisque causing a thick layer of glaze to adhere. Wipe the surface before glazing for a thinner glaze layer, but if the surface is too wet, the glaze may run off the bisque resulting in a thin or uneven distribution of glaze.

- The best sponges for glazing are the large wall-paper sponges sold at building supply stores. These sponges have small pores and are excel-lent for wiping wet glaze off pots. A large-pore sponge doesn't last as long and leaves uneven edges when wiping a glazed surface.

- If you need to wipe glaze off your pot, do it im-mediately while the glaze is still wet. Wet glaze comes off easier and quicker and causes less staining than if you waited until the glaze was dry on the pot.

Recipes

Warm Jade Green
Cone 6

Whiting.	16.0 %
Ferro Frit 3124.	9.0
Talc.	9.0
Custer Feldspar	40.0
EPK Kaolin.	10.0
Silica	16.0
	100.0 %
Add: Copper Carbonate.	4.0 %
Rutile	6.0 %

Licorice Black
Cone 6

Whiting.	4.0 %
Ferro Frit 3134.	26.0
Custer Feldspar	22.0
Talc.	5.0
EPK Kaolin.	17.0
Silica	26.0
	100.0 %
Add: Cobalt Carbonate	2.0 %
Red Iron Oxide	9.0 %

Shelly's Blue
Cone 6
by Michelle Bonior

Dolomite	4.0 %
Whiting.	6.0
Zinc Oxide	4.0
Custer Feldspar	47.0
Gillespie Borate	13.0
EPK Kaolin.	3.0
Silica	23.0
	100.0 %
Add: Rutile	2.0 %
Copper Carbonate.	1.5 %
Cobalt Carbonate	0.5 %
Bentonite	2.0 %

Strong, Pure and Matt

by Patrick Horstley

Squared bowl, lidded jar, boat vase with 1911 Purple/Blue glaze and wax. Fan vase and spiral platter with 1879 Rust Red.

I'm an avid experimenter, exploring specific materials to achieve new colors and unusual glaze surfaces, or just trying new ideas. There are many variations available by just exchanging feldspars or clays—EPK Kaolin for ball clay, #6 Tile for EPK Kaolin—the list is endless. The glaze notebook I'm using now contains up to 3000 glaze tests!

I want my glaze colors to be strong, pure and matt in surface to produce sharp graphic patterns, and I prefer glazes that absorb rather than reflect the light. My technique for glazing is a wax-resist process. First, I spray a colored glaze on a piece using a Geil HVLP spray gun. Next, I often draw images of the Oregon landscape with a soft pencil, then the drawn area is covered with liquid wax. When the wax is dry (usually a couple of hours), I cut it away and glaze to make the pattern I want on the pot. I then dip the piece in a silver black glaze so that the glazes meet edge to edge.

All my work is bisque fired to cone 08 and glaze fired to cone 6 in reduction. Cone 6 saves gas and time, and as the work has become more sculptural, the cone 6 clays tend to be better because they don't move around in the firing. I've been able to duplicate most cone 10 glazes at cone 6 with some testing. Even after many years of making pots, on most days I can't wait to be in the studio.

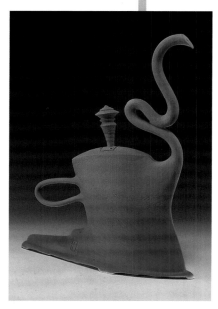

Teapot, 22 inches in height, thrown and altered with extruded parts, 1911 Purple/Blue under 1631 Aqua.

Press-molded vase, with porcelain slip and wax pattern under 1134C Matt Black.

Recipes

1911 Purple/Blue
Cone 6 Reduction
Barium Carbonate	40.0 %
Custer Feldspar	40.0
C&C Ball Clay	2.0
EPK Kaolin	18.0
	100.0 %
Add: Copper Carbonate	6.0 %

1204 Purple/Blue
Cone 6 Reduction
Barium Carbonate	50.0 %
Zinc	10.0
Nepheline Syenite	20.0
C&C Ball Clay	15.0
EPK Kaolin	5.0
	100.0 %
Add: Copper Carbonate	2.5 %

1631 Aqua
Cone 6 Reduction
Barium Carbonate	47.5 %
Nepheline Syenite	47.5
Pemco Frit P-626	5.0
	100.0 %
Add: Bentonite	4.0 %
Copper Carbonate	9.0 %

1879 Rust Red
Cone 6 Reduction
Whiting	28.6 %
Custer Feldspar	17.8
EPK Kaolin	53.6
	100.0 %
Add: Ferro Frit 3134	10.0 %
Tricalcium Phosphate	4.0 %
Red Iron Oxide	4.0 %

1134C Matt Black
Cone 6 Reduction
Barium Carbonate	41.0 %
Lithium Carbonate	6.0
Nepheline Syenite	20.0
EPK Kaolin	20.0
Silica	11.0
Bentonite	2.0
	100.0 %
Add: Red Iron Oxide	2.0 %
Manganese Dioxide	2.0 %
Cobalt Carbonate	2.0 %
Chrome Oxide	2.0 %

1634 Shino
Cone 6 Reduction
Aluminum Oxide (A-12)	55.0 %
Soda Ash	5.0
Nepheline Syenite	30.0
Spodumene	5.0
Bentonite	5.0
	100.0 %

Rollie Younger
Boiler Teapots

by Lauren Zolot Younger

"High (pressure) Tea," 14½ inches in height, thrown, extruded and assembled stoneware, with sprayed Bronze Glaze, fired to cone 5–6, with metal gauge.

"Industrial Strength Tea," 14 inches in height, with sprayed Bronze Glaze, fired to cone 5–6, with metal gauge and stand.

On the gentle coast of central California, Rollie Younger creates his industrial teapots in a place where all the pressure of the industrial world is very far removed from daily life.

In his studio, Younger works late into the night, listening to blues and experimenting with shapes. Spreading out thrown and extruded shapes, he uses a putty knife and pieces of driftwood to incise or impose ridges. The shapes sometimes seem uneventful on their own, but when the extrusions meet up with the thrown forms, they attract each other.

"When I cut off the bottoms of the cylinders and stacked them, I was reminded of the old-fashioned boilers I'd find at the fish canneries in Monterey." In order to create the sensation of a boiler, Younger paid close attention to the symbols that read as metal, such as rivets, banding and welding marks. Each teapot also has a condenser-like shape on the spout.

The cylinders are wheel thrown, and the handles and spouts are ex-

Rollie Younger attaching a pressure gauge to a finished teapot.

truded. The cylinders are assembled, then the handles are added, followed by the bridges. The bridges connect the spouts to the teapot body. Welding marks are made at each point of connection, and rivets are applied last. The dark-metal finish of each body is a sprayed Bronze Glaze from Cuesta College, fired to cone 5 in oxidation. The rivets are either painted with bronze enamel or are bronze luster fired to cone 017. Some of the teapots sit on metal stands forged by Mecki Heussen, a friend and metal artist. Other pieces sit directly on a surface, looking very much like Russian samovars (copper urns used for tea), and range in size from 1 to 2 feet tall.

To further pique the interest of the viewer, Younger attaches pres-sure gauges and copper fittings to certain pieces. The gauges are fixed into the crowns with epoxy. The repeated roundness of the rivets, connector holes and gauges creates an organic quality that contrasts with the seemingly metallic sculpture. The curves of the extruded handles and spouts add to the effect.

Younger's teapots hold much more than tea. They reflect the personality of a culture. This is what Younger has found in his travels, from the village potters of Japan to the studio of Michael Cardew in England and the countryside potters of Denmark. Having explored these different cultures' shapes, techniques and attitudes, he has developed a sense of culture himself. His boiler teapots reflect the pressure of industrial life, where breaks are short and surroundings are efficient. However, inside the pieces is a colorful glaze that is surprising for its contrast with the outside, reflecting the beauty and spirit inside us all. "The boiler teapots seemed to grow and flow with their own energy," Younger stated. "The details came from intuition. I had no preconceived plan but got swept up in pure creative pleasure, and that's a great space to be in."

Younger's love of industrial design, and fascination with functional whimsy, comes from the era and environment in which he grew up— 1950s Los Angeles. Life revolved around his father's tools and machines, piles of mechanical and automotive parts that only five brothers could accumulate, and a love for art that was inspired by teachers and an older brother.

Besides being a studio potter, Younger has taught ceramics for 22 years in both high school and junior college. He provides an arena for exploring creativity and personal development, inspiring his students to go beyond the fundamentals.

"I've always been fascinated with teapots—the shapes, the forms. On one hand, a teapot keeps me grounded, because it needs to hold water and pour properly without dripping. It is an everyday item that can remind its user of the joy, humor and beauty in life. I like the fact that people use art in an everyday way when they use their teapots. On the other hand, a teapot allows me to leap from functional to nonfunctional. If it has a handle and a spout, it's a teapot. This permits me to explore the inner space and outer surface, extending the physical limits of its use or symbology. The fact that it's a teapot is pleasure enough."

The shapes of these teapots draw the viewer in to inquire and investigate. They are familiar symbols from industry, but when sculpted in clay, they become beautiful on their own terms. The pots make one want to pick them up and look inside. The gauges and copper fittings inspire curiosity, and make people smile with wonder and delight.

If a pun can be withstood: These pots are ironic. Though they look hard, like iron, there is a softness and pleasure that is apparent in these teapots.

"Green Tea," 13 inches in height, thrown and assembled, with sprayed copper green glaze, fired to cone 5–6, with copper tubing and metal stand.

19

"Turbo Tea," 14 inches in height, thrown and assembled stoneware with sprayed Bronze Glaze, fired to cone 5–6, with metal, stand and handle, by Rollie Younger.

Recipes

Bronze Glaze

Cone 5–6

Manganese Dioxide	39.0 %
Cedar Heights Redart	52.4
Kentucky OM 4 Ball Clay	4.3
Silica	4.3
	100.0 %
Add: Cobalt Carbonate	2.7 %
Copper Oxide	4.3 %

A medium/thin application yields a matt gold. Extreme care should be taken while working with manganese dioxide. A NIOSH-approved respirator with a HEPA (high-efficiency particulate air) filter should be worn, and kilns should be vented to remove all fumes during firing.

Red Glaze

Cone 6

Gerstley Borate	21.0 %
Whiting	20.0
Nepheline Syenite	16.0
EPK Kaolin	11.0
Silica	32.0
	100.0 %
Add: Tin Oxide	5.0 %
Chrome Oxide	0.2 %

A thick application turns this glaze mauve or purple. Best when fired in an electric kiln. Any reduction in the atmosphere turns this glaze pink.

Susan Beiner
Too Much Is Not Enough

by Billie Sessions

"Fruitful," 9 inches in height, slip-cast and assembled porcelain, with glazes and lusters, multiple firings.

When Susan Beiner speaks about her library, she is not talking about books. She is talking about molds of found objects and forms created from her imagination that she squeezes onto a variety of forms to create a dazzling wealth of visual energy. Beiner usually has about 200 molds at any given time. These forms are her library, and thus her vocabulary.

Just as vocabulary can change in different settings, so too does Beiner's choice of forms used on her surfaces. She is constantly search-ing for new "words" to alter her message. And her message changes quite frequently, from colossal wall pieces dripping with shells, fruit-like forms, giant hooks and bolts to tropical leaves and petite amalgam-ated succulents resembling precious bubble-ringed, cheery artichokes. When she completes an oversized porcelain-encrusted wall piece filled with thousands of molded shapes, or a sizeable assemblage of fruity, elfinlike works, she throws out those molds, forcing herself to find and create a new vocabulary.

**"Screw Teapot," 8½ inches in height,
slip-cast and assembled porcelain, with luster.**

Though Beiner is possibly most known for her "Screw Teapots," overflowing with hardware like a tool man's wet dream, she has abandoned these since her move to Southern California. It's apparent that the screw pots were a direct response to the industry of the Detroit neighborhood where she lived and worked from 1994 to 2000. Beiner's work is proof that the Motor City is a playground for an artist interested in industrial items. "Hardware elements started there because it was so industrial. For instance, my studio was in an old building where they used to make airplane parts."

Two of her artist friends utilized scrap metal in their work and Beiner would rummage through their heaps of "junk" and find things that she would then use as molded objects. She was appropriating the heart and history of Detroit into art. "For me, it was taking what was old and discarded and presenting it in

a new way. I was translating the traditional to the fantastic." Even though most of her new vocabulary these days is based on imaginary, organic forms that she molds from what she sees in her new sun-filled environment, she admits she will always use hardware. She claims it's the vocabulary word she will never abandon.

Beiner's true passion is sumptuous surfaces. Too much is not enough. Throughout the years, she has been encouraged to change her opulent and profuse casings. However, her studio mate in Detroit, Kathy Dambach, was influential in convincing Beiner to stick with it and work through her ideas. "When I began working," Beiner recalls, "my style wasn't accepted much and it took some time for people to get used to the energy. I am a workaholic and have the energy to keep working and to be fearless. I enjoy the time and the challenge of what the work presents. The intensity of the surface and color gets me going."

Beiner's encrusted work is naturally thought to have its aesthetic roots in Bernard Palissy's work. Yet, she was unaware of his work until her surfaces were well on their way to their present state of congestion. All the same, some of her influences are clearly explainable. It turns out that her childhood home in New Jersey played an important role. Since her mother loved fine china, her father would bring indigenous ceramic tokens home from various parts of the world where he trav-

"New Hybrid #3," 7 inches in height, slip-cast and assembled porcelain, with glazes, fired to cone 6.

eled for work. Over the years, the breakfront cabinet became filled with cups and saucers of completely diverse designs, colors and surfaces. Beiner cherished these rowdy bits and pieces.

Years later, as a ceramics student, Beiner was drawn to studying festooned silverware and bejeweled Meissen and Sèvres pieces, noting their parallel surface adornments. She is well aware that these styles peaked her intuitive cravings, having always been drawn to active surfaces. Until recently, she was constantly reviewing her reference

"Klubbo," 20 inches in diameter, slip-cast and assembled porcelain, with glazes, fired to cone 6, with aluminum.

books about 18th-century vessel forms and their purposes, since she was translating those forms and their flamboyant decoration into her contemporary encrustations.

As a painting major at Rutgers University, Beiner enrolled in ceramics her junior year. She became acquainted with the possibilities of molds from Lynn Peters who was a graduate student. Beiner stayed an extra year, completing her B.F.A. in ceramics. She knew this was the tip of the iceberg, as far as what she needed to apply for a terminal degree in ceramics. She relocated to Arizona State University to prepare.

Uprooting herself again, she moved to Ann Arbor, Michigan for an M.F.A. Next, she moved to Detroit to begin concentrated studio work as adjunct faculty for the College for Creative Studies (CCS) at the College of Art and Design. Her mentor there was Tom Phardel. He was adventurous about experimenting with new glazes, surface orientations and techniques. Teaching slip casting for five years at CCS taught Beiner an enthusiastic and disciplined zeal for the potential of using molds to satisfy her vocabulary.

She is now teaching art at California State University, San Bernardino. "For the first two years in California, I was out of my mind. I made the last screw teapot here . . . , but I wasn't sure where it would lead. The series was over, as my environment had changed. Southern California was so different than any place I had ever been. I started thinking about not making pots anymore and making sculpture instead. I questioned what it was to make sculpture. It's a whole different set of principles. I haven't made any teapots for over a year now and I like the idea that I don't have to limit myself. I really think that all the years that I made teapots were somewhat limiting, just because I didn't really know that I could not make them. Although I am still interested in the vessel form, now it's completely nonfunctional."

Forms unfold from her sketchbook. They may not have a direct historical connection like the objects that she was making in the 1980s and 1990s.

"New Hybrids," to 7 inches in height each, slip-cast and assembled porcelain, with glazes, fired to cone 6.

Before, she was sketching traditional forms and attaching castings of found objects. Presently, she uses her sketchbook to record, translate and develop her own forms. This new approach is more engaging for her. The only time that she uses found objects is for the hardware elements in her work. However, the size of the hardware has increased. Beiner has found hardware suppliers that allow her to borrow and return their pricy industrial hooks, bolts and screws.

Because of Beiner's energy and her confession that she gets bored easily, it makes sense that her work evolves relatively rapidly from one articulation of her vocabulary to another. Beiner is translating the landscape of indigenous succulents of southern California. This latest evolution of her structural design vocabulary she calls "New Hybrids." These have evolved from last year's "Hybrids." More diminutive than the others, they are about 7 inches in height, composed of two pieces. They are action-packed pinnacles set on a saucerlike form with a concerted relationship of color and texture. They are sumptuous, like the experience of driving past fragrant orange groves. With Beiner's flair for the ornate, a cactus is translated into a cluster of energetic, pineapplelike agricultural matter, twisting with bold and festive color combinations, overloaded with shells, ping-pong balls, nubbins, screws and such. Characteristically for Beiner's passionate need to stuff a space, she will fill a whole wall full of these embryonic buddies.

"The difference between what I did before and the new work is that I'm working sculpturally with the inside space of the cast parts. In other words, I am casting the pieces that frequently resemble an improbable leaf or bud and working with the interiors of the casts. I am interested in altering the form because it gives me more options. I can be playful as I investigate the interior space by cutting them open. They move in space, rather than being static. I can manipulate, cut, form and reassemble parts using a multitude of methods—allowing each piece to blossom. I am dealing with interchangeable parts, and I need to move all the combinations around until I find the appropriate feel. Then they come alive for me. I can't figure them out until I can play around with them."

Prior to the "New Hybrids," Beiner never used crusty glazes or put matt, satin or gloss glazes together on one piece. She is now experimenting with layering them. "I have always been a color freak, so for me to play with the relationship of color to surface this much and have it all together in a small space is a new puzzle. It's like a design problem—integrating an idea strictly through color and shape." As she views two long rows of these pieces, looking like a furrowed crop ready to be picked and taken to market, she says, "Though this group looks somewhat like repetition, I consider all of these as one piece. I'm going to make more, because I am experimenting with a lot of new things that I haven't done before. I am continually developing new fluid colors to add to my palette so I can examine the activity as the colors interact with one another on these pieces. I want a highly smooth surface so the layers of color will ooze on that form—so luscious you might want to lick them."

When asked what Beiner would do to a living room if she had all the time in the world to make it her own, she replied "I would make ceramic wallpaper that would extend out from the walls. The room would be a historical encrustation of objects from my life. I would have thick glass shelves placed within the wallpaper, each holding a specific object from the people in my life. It's all about activity and celebration—a massive encrustation."

"Hybrid #3," 25 inches in height, slip-cast and assembled porcelain, with glazes, by Susan Beiner.

Color: Cones 6 through 10

Beiner gets these brilliant colors in firings to cone 6 or 10. She doesn't like the look of low-fired glazes, as they are not dense enough for her color palette. She likes the look of china or porcelain and has created a low-grade porcelain slip with a lot of ball clay. Because she is interested in making color more intense, she makes her stains as bright as possible by putting an opaque white matt glaze underneath the colored gloss glaze. The opaque white glaze is fired to cone 10, but the colored glaze is fired to cone 6–7. The colored glaze melts into the higher-fired glaze, permitting her to fire it anywhere between cone 6 and cone 10. The glaze is applied quite thick, thicker than she teaches her students to apply glazes. It doesn't run because the glaze underneath is not fluxed at cone 6, though it starts fluxing at cone 8. She sprays the colors on, which requires a lot of wax to separate the colors and textures. Since too much is not enough, it's only natural that all of Beiner's projects, large or small, involve incalculable hours of glazing.

Surprisingly, Beiner has found a limit to her time-consuming obsessions. She doesn't clean mold seams, as she is fond of the added texture they give her pieces. She refuses to score when attaching add-ons. Instead, she attaches parts with a "goop" made from her casting slip, combined with Epsom salts. The slip is deflocculated and the Epsom salts (magnesium sulfate) flocculates it. It acts like Velcro! She adds 2 tablespoons of Epsom salts to a cup of water, then heats up the water to dissolve the salts. She then adds 1 tablespoon of this mixture to a quart of slip and it stiffens quickly. She loves the fat edge that the "goop" gives her when it hangs out from under her hordes of fabrications.

William Sawhill
Crystalline Glazes

by Howard Sawhill

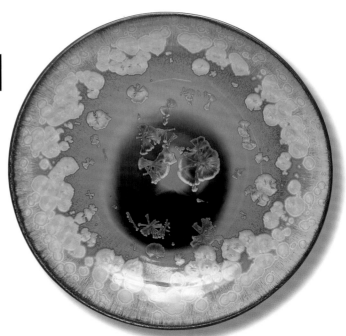

Plate, 15 inches in diameter, porcelain/stoneware blend, Crystalline Glaze with iron and cobalt, fired to cone 10 in oxidation.

Carefully studying the intricacies and variations of every square inch of one of his ceramic vases, Bill Sawhill finds the one small area where the glaze acts in perfect harmony. He looks up at me and says, "Now, if only we could make the whole piece like this area here." While most potters accept the variability in glaze appearance as part of the magic of the firing process, Sawhill has spent more than 25 years perfecting glaze colors and textures and reducing what he deemed "flaws" in the glazes. The result of this quest has been the creation of a crystalline reduction glazing technique that produces beautifully warm-toned crystalline glazes.

Himself the son of a painter by avocation, Sawhill's sensitive eye for color developed in his 20s and 30s as a paint formulator for an industrial paint company. Our family remembers the warm salmon color he cooked up just for our dining room. His last five years with the paint company took our family to Antwerp, Belgium, where he worked as technical advisor to common mar-

ket licensees. During the latter half of his 30-year career, he learned the science of ceramic dispersions working as a formulator of magnetic tapes. It's a special feeling knowing that some of my early-year conversations are captured on audiotapes developed by my father.

Sawhill's introduction to pottery came in 1970 on a trip to visit my sister Sue at the University of California, Berkeley. We had stopped off at Leslie Ceramic Supply to look for some supplies for my high-school art class when my father spotted a build-it-yourself wooden kick wheel. He thought it would be fun for us to put together. Back at home, we loaded up the flywheel with bricks, tightened a bunch of nuts and, before we knew it, had ourselves a working potter's wheel. Next, we built a raku kiln inside a 55-gallon drum using a burner we rummaged from our local heating and air-conditioning repair store. I spent the next several years making small pieces and selling them to neighbors for movie money.

Sawhill's personal interest in ceramics began when I went off to college to study ceramics and left him with shelves full of glaze chemicals. By the time I returned home from my first semester, the garage had become his ceramics studio, complete with a new electric wheel. His first phase was small functional ware. He worked for months designing a well-balanced, pleasant-to-hold, non-leaking coffee cup. I still have one of these cherished cups on my desk at work. Satisfied with the sound results of his coffee-cup designs, Sawhill turned his attention to making jars and vases. His fall project for many years was making jelly jars, which were then filled with mom's garden-fresh, home-made blackberry jam, offered as presents to friends and neighbors. He experimented with celadon and sang-de-boeuf glazes in his cone 10 oxidation kiln, and added teapots to his list of pieces. As with many new potters, most of his early wheel-made pieces were under 9 inches in height. Armed with increasing encouragement from his family (who formerly referred to his vases as short and dumpy) and a useful trade secret (no one knows how much you trim), Sawhill entered his large-functional-ware phase. He began making tall, feather-light vases and decorating them with experimental glazes. He soon reached the limit of how tall he could make a flower vase that was still practical and began turning his big pieces into lamps. He started selling these lamps at regional ceramics shows and joined several area cooperative art galler-

ies, where he worked several days a month selling different kinds of art along with his own pieces.

His need for more firing capacity led him to design and build a gas kiln. When the bricks came, we laid them out in the garage to decide how large to make the floor. He was definitely thinking big, but after moving bricks around for a couple hours, we settled on a design approximately 4×6 feet (down from the 10×10 feet he had originally imagined). He had a local welder make the frame and he ordered special wheels to carry the weight.

It is at this point that Sawhill turned his energy to working with

Bowl, 14 inches in diameter, porcelain/stoneware blend, Crystalline Glaze with manganese, cobalt and iron, fired to cone 10.

Bud vase, 4 inches in height, porcelain/stoneware blend, Crystalline Glaze with iron, fired to cone 10 in oxidation.

crystalline glazes, a glaze family known best for its inherent irreproducibility. He began with the base recipe from Diane Creber, which was based on a recipe from David Snair and made his first pieces with crystals. He found that, if he worked with bowls instead of vases, only half of the glaze would run off onto his kiln shelf, allowing the other half to flow into the bowl and crack. He started playing around with the recipe and found that spodumene reduced the tendency for cracking in thick areas, as would feldspar, but without reducing crystal formation. He used bentonite to help reduce the settling, and there was a slight smell of vinegar in his glaze,

which he claimed was wine added for character.

He noticed that crystals tended to form only in the thickest parts of the glaze, leading to plates and bowls with crystals concentrated at the center sections and vases with crystals congregating near the foot or lower neck. In order to reduce the tendency of glazes to run during firing, he developed a magnesium-rich flow-control glaze, which he applied to the piece prior to the crystalline glaze. This yielded somewhat more evenly distributed crystals, but the glaze had a tendency to crater on internal surfaces where the glaze pooled.

To prevent the glaze from running onto his kiln shelves, he made catch basins for each piece. They were shaped like candlesticks, where the cylindrical section was matched in diameter to the foot of the main piece. After bisque firing, he attached these two pieces together with wood glue to hold them together for glazing. As the glaze flowed to the bottom of the piece during firing, it would continue to flow along the catch-basin cylinder and flow into the reservoir of the basin, instead of onto the kiln shelf. After the glaze firing, he used a diamond stylus to scribe around the circumference of the joint and, with a careful tap of a hammer and chisel, carefully separated the piece from the basin. He ground the foot smooth on a diamond-faced disc mounted on his potter's wheel.

To put more color in his glazes, Sawhill chose a roughly 50/50 mixture of a celadon and crackle glaze, found in Joseph Grebanier's book *Chinese Stoneware Glazes*, to which he added 10–20% oxide colorants. Among his favorite additives were manganese dioxide, copper carbonate, cobalt carbonate and colorants that (although no longer officially in existence) he had squirreled away from his earlier days in industrial labs. He preferred carbonates of copper and cobalt for their superior color development. Nickel oxide gave vivid colors, but he thought it interfered with the crystal formation. Applying this glaze over the crystalline glaze allowed the oxides to be picked up and redistributed through the crystal glaze during firing.

Sawhill added a third, very thin, refractory glaze layer made from the colorant glaze with 10% zinc oxide added to help control the glaze flow (he called this a barrier layer glaze). To ensure an even coating of this thin outer glaze application, he added a very small amount of red iron oxide, which enabled him to see the pink color as the glaze was sprayed on.

His typical firing started at 9 PM and used an overnight heating cycle to cone 10, followed by a cooling and four-hour crystal-growing cycle at cone 04–05. By noon the next day, the kiln was cool enough to open. He pointed out that the peak electrical rates in his area ran from noon to 6 PM. This firing cycle saved him a quarter of the peak electricity costs.

Sawhill spent several years producing crystalline-glazed pieces with green and blue tones. His specialty became plates and vases. He discov-

Recipes

Crystalline Glaze
Cone 10

Titanium Dioxide	7.8 %
Zinc Oxide	23.4
Spodumene	1.5
Ferro Frit 3110	45.8
Bentonite	1.5
EPK Kaolin	1.5
Silica	18.5
	100.0 %

A modified David Snair glaze.

Colorant Glaze
Cone 10

Magnesium Carbonate	2.3 %
Whiting	20.4
Buckingham Feldspar	38.6
Georgia Kaolin	14.3
Silica	24.5
	100.0 %

Add 10–20% ceramic stains.

Barrier Layer Glaze
Cone 10

Magnesium Carbonate	2.1 %
Whiting	18.6
Zinc Oxide	9.1
Buckingham Feldspar	35.0
Georgia Kaolin	13.0
Silica	22.2
	100.0 %

Add 0.5% red iron oxide to give pink tint.

Flower vase, 10 inches in height, porcelain/stoneware blend, Crystalline Glaze with manganese, fired in reduction to cone 10, by William Sawhill.

ered that small plates sold very well, but he thought the larger plates showed off his crystals better. He designed a number of plaster molds over which he draped slabs of clay in order to make his larger plates. He began to explore the reduction process as a means to introduce different colors. He took pieces fired to cone 10 in oxidation and fired them a second time in reduction. Early explosions led to many very nice shards and inspired him to make crystalline-glazed earrings as gifts to those who purchased his pieces. He used to joke that his earrings were selling more pottery pieces than he was. Many explosions later, he discovered that he could heat the kiln slowly to about 1292°F, reduce the pieces for just under an hour, and achieve the unique warm-toned crystalline glazes that became his hallmark.

Making Crystals Clear

by Sumi von Dassow

The most fascinating and exacting glaze family of all may be the crystalline glazes. Achieving and controlling the growth of crystals in molten glaze is as close to pure science as pottery gets. To most of us, it remains an obscure and mysterious science with rules we don't really understand but results we admire mightily.

The Challenges

Crystalline glazes are difficult to work with for two major reasons: First, crystals grow only in a glaze that is very low in alumina, which makes these glazes very fluid when they melt. Thus, a major challenge for users of crystalline glazes is controlling the glaze flow so it doesn't get all over the kiln shelves. This is usually done by firing each pot on its own pedestal with a built-in catch basin for the overflow of glaze.

The second challenging aspect of working with crystalline glazes is that, to grow crystals, the glaze must be fired to its melting temperature, partially cooled, then held at the optimum crystal-growing temperature for several hours. The firing

schedule can be varied in a number of ways to achieve different results, but firing crystalline glazes requires a pyrometer and constant attention to the temperature inside the kiln or a computer-controlled kiln with a pyrometer.

A Hardy Soul

These hurdles mean relatively few potters venture into crystalline territory. Carla Thorpe is one of those hardy souls. Carla, formerly a jeweler, since taking up pottery has been attracted to time-consuming techniques that allow her to lose herself for hours in the process of making a pot. She has eagerly embraced the challenge of crystalline glazes, both because she enjoys the process and because in growing crystals on a pot she is literally mimicking the process that created many of the gemstones she used to work with. Though the loss rate can be high, and preparing and finishing the pots can be tedious, she is endlessly fascinated by the results.

The blue crystals on this blue jar are formed from cobalt oxide while the blue background results from the cobalt carbonate.

Carla's Technique: The Barrier

During a recent visit to her studio, Carla demonstrated the processes of preparing a pot for glazing and applying a glaze, and of separating fired pots from their catch-basin pedestals and grinding the foot smooth. Preparing a pot for glazing simply requires gluing the pot to its pedestal with a mixture of white glue and alumina hydrate, preferably the day before glazing so the glue can dry. The glue keeps the pot precisely placed on the pedestal during glazing and loading so that the runny glaze won't seep under the pot in the firing and adhere it permanently to the pedestal. The alumina hydrate forms a barrier between the pot and pedestal after the glue burns away, so they can be separated easily along the seam between the two pieces.

Glaze Application

Carla applies glaze by brushing it on liberally with a large soft Japanese "hake" brush. Crystalline glazes can be difficult to apply, since they can't contain any clay. In most glazes, clay is used not only to provide needed minerals but also to keep glazes from settling quickly and to facilitate application of a smooth even coat either by brushing or dipping. Unfortunately, clay contains alumina and so can't be used in crystalline glazes. Fortunately, the extremely fluid nature of the glaze means that the glaze can be "slopped on," as Carla puts it, in a messy and uneven coat and it will smooth out in the firing. She also notes that these glazes change consistency over time and many potters only mix up enough for one day's work. To most potters this would represent another tedious aspect to crystalline glazing, but to Carla it presents an opportunity to experiment with many different combinations of glaze colorants.

Firing

The firing process is exacting but fairly simple if you have a computer-controlled kiln. She uses the schedule recommended by the kiln manufacturer (Skutt) for crystalline glazes.

Cleaning the Bases

After the pots are cool, the next tedious part of the process is separating the pots from their pedestals

Segment	Ramp/Hour	Set Point	Hold Time
1	200°F/Hour	800°F	0
2	150°F/Hour	1250°F	0
3	300°F/Hour	2100°F	0
4	108°F/Hour	2330°F	0
5	999°F/Hour	2050°F	3 hours

Carla often varies this schedule by dropping the temperature to 2000°F degrees three times, then immediately increasing it to 2050°F and holding it for an hour each time. This schedule promotes the formation of "growth rings" in the crystals.

Segment	Ramp/Hour	Set Point	Hold Time
Repeat previous steps 1–4 then:			
5	999°F/Hour*	2000°F	0
6	999°F/Hour*	2050°F	1 hour
7	999°F/Hour*	2000°F	0
8	999°F/Hour*	2050°F	1 hour
9	999°F/Hour*	2000°F	0

* "999°" refers to full-on or full-off power. This setting varies among different controllers so check your owners manual.

and grinding the bottom smooth. Carla performs the separating operation with a hammer and chisel; other potters use a Dremel tool with a grinding bit. For grinding the bottom smooth, Carla uses a bench grinder left over from her jewelry days, which is equipped with an exhaust fan, a very nice feature. She uses a fine-textured grinding disk manufactured specifically for the purpose of grinding glaze drips. Carla explains that some potters finish their crystalline glazed pots by gluing them onto wooden pedestals to cover up the imperfect foot, but she prefers to grind the bottom as smooth as possible and leave it bare. If the pot was fired on a carefully fitted pedestal, this is not too difficult.

A Star Performance

Those pots that survive all this stressful treatment come out with beautiful glossy coats embellished with crystals of varying colors, like captured snowflakes. They are stunning, particularly when seen in bright sunlight. At first one's eye takes in the sparkling effect of the pot as a whole, then it begins to see the galaxy-like swirl of crystals with-in the glaze. Gradually the eye is drawn deeper into the glaze, eventually examining and marveling at the structure of the individual crystals. It is this irresistible attraction that makes these glazes star performers.

Recipes

Snair Crystalline Glaze Variation
Cone 9

Ferro Frit 3110.	49.3 %
Zinc oxide	24.8
Kaolin	1.5
Silica	18.3
Titanium dioxide	6.1
	100.0 %
Add: Bentonite	1.0 %

Cream colors
Red iron oxide.	1.0 %
Manganese dioxide.	0.5 %

Blues
Cobalt oxide	2.0 %
Cobalt carbonate	2.0 %
Manganese dioxide.	3.0 %

Developing Crystals at Mid Range

by William Schran

Four vessels, to 8 inches in height, thrown B-Mix clay. Glazes are as follows. Left to right: Fa's Cone 6 Base (Revised) glaze with 3% manganese dioxide and .5% cobalt carbonate; MFE (Dan Turnidge Revised) glaze with 3% manganese dioxide and 1% cobalt carbonate; Fa's Cone 6 Base glaze revised with 3% manganese dioxide and .5% cobalt carbonate; and MFE (Dan Turnidge Revised) glaze with 3% manganese dioxide and 1% cobalt carbonate.

My fascination with macro-crystalline glazes began as a graduate student. While visiting a local exhibition of an individual's collection, I discovered two small porcelain bottles by Herbert Sanders. The glazes appeared to have blue colored snowflakes frozen on a transparent sky of orange. From that initial encounter, macrocrystalline glazing has become a process that I've revisited many times over the years.

Sanders had published *Glazes for Special Effects* in 1974, which contained recipes for crystalline glazes. In 1976, I began experimenting with several recipes listed in the book, but since it was difficult to fire our electric kilns to the required cone 9–10 temperature range, I had little success. An article by David Snair in *Ceramics Monthly* provided additional glaze recipes and techniques for preparing the pots for firing. Though all the recipes were for cone 9, a comment in the article stated

that firing to cone 6 would also produce crystals. I had some limited success with these glazes, but that comment stuck in my head.

Fast forward to 1994. Discussions of glazes with a group of my students lead to a question about crystalline glazes. This one question resulted in a semester-long series of glaze tests that resulted in few successes. It was the problem I had encountered years before, our electric kilns only reached cone 9–10 with much difficulty. The lack of success producing crystals by my students only strengthened my resolve to find a solution. It was then, that I recalled the Snair article and the comment about cone 6.

With additional information gathered through Internet searches and interlibrary loans, I discovered some artists experimenting with crystalline glazes at lower temperatures. Since we conducted our glaze firings to cone 6 at school, I decided to target this temperature for my testing.

My initial experiments involved firing cone 10 glaze recipes only to cone 6. These tests resulted in the discovery that crystalline glazes could be produced in this lower temperature range by simply introducing additional fluxes. The flux that seemed to produce the best results was lithium carbonate. Other materials that would function as a powerful flux were either soluble or contained additional silica and alumina, which are not desirable in crystalline glazes.

All of my experiments with crystalline glaze firings, up until fall 2006, have been done in a manually operated electric kiln. The kiln has infinite controls, so with careful monitoring, I was able to control the firing schedule fairly accurately. A digital pyrometer is an essential tool to closely track temperature changes, especially during long holding cycles. Acquisition of my first kiln with a programmable controller has allowed for more complicated, repeatable firing schedules. The ability to be able to alter temperature ramp speeds and specific temperature hold times have opened up new avenues of experimentation. I have also found that, for both types of kilns, a direct vent system is important for rapid cooling cycles and maintaining an oxidizing atmosphere.

Crystalline Technique

I've developed techniques through years of experimentation, adopting processes that worked, eliminating those that produced only limited success. Web searches and recent publications provide a variety of approaches to this very involved process, and each individual need to conduct tests to find the process that makes the most sense for his or her particular circumstances.

Crystalline glazes produce the best results when applied to a smooth white clay body. Many artisans work with a porcelain clay body. Porcelain comes with its own set of issues and I have found a cone 10 porcelaneous stoneware clay—B-Mix or Bee-Mix—that works very well with my glazes. I chose to use a cone 10 clay to reduce the amount of alumina that might be picked up by the glaze.

A normal glaze has a mix of silica/flux/alumina in a ratio that provides a glassy surface and remains in place when melted on a vertical surface. A crystalline glaze contains little or no alumina, which would inhibit crystal growth. The glaze is comprised of silica, flux and a saturation of zinc oxide. This highly fluxed mix of materials leads to a very fluid glaze and steps must be taken to avoid destroying kiln shelves or the kiln.

Catch Basins and Pedestals

Every pot must have its own catch plate/basin to contain the glaze that runs off the pot. The catch plate need not be made from the same clay as the pot. The plate can be wheel thrown or hand built. Each pot must also have some type of pedestal device to facilitate removal of the pot after firing. Some potters use insulating firebrick to create the pedestal. The brick must be at least a

Crystalline glazes run off the pot so you need to raise the piece on a pedestal that sits in a catch basin. It's important to select a pedestal that closely matches the diameter of the foot. Preparing several sizes allows you to select one with the correct fit.

Apply three to four coats of glaze to achieve the desired thickness, brushing each layer in a different direction.

Pieces ready to load in the kiln. Each glazed pot is positioned on a pedestal that is placed in a catch basin.

After the firing, the fluid glaze will have run down over the pedestal and into the catch basin.

2600K-type and coated with kiln wash. Another technique involves throwing the pedestal from the same clay body as the pot. After bisque firing, the pedestal is attached to the pot with a mix of white glue, which holds the pedestal in place before firing, and kaolin, which acts as a separating agent after firing. Striking with a sharp chisel or heating with a small torch just below the joint with the pot removes the pedestal. After encountering a number of problems with each of these methods, such as pots falling over or broken foot rings, I sought another solution. Ellie Blair, a fellow crystalline artist, provided this process to me—the

The pedestal and catch basin are removed by tapping with a small chisel along the line where the pedestal joins the pot.

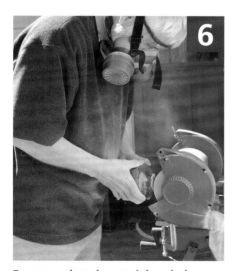

Excess pedestal material and glaze are ground off the bottom using a bench grinder fitted with a silicon carbide grinding wheel.

pedestals are a mix of equal parts by volume: alumina, kaolin and sawdust. Add just enough water to bind the materials and form the mix into ¾-inch thick "biscuits" cut to the foot diameter of the bisque fired pot using round cookie cutters. I've found this material to stand up well to the

melting glaze and soft enough to be easily knocked off with a chisel. Any remaining pedestal is easily ground away from the pot.

Glaze Application

Crystalline glazes may be applied like most other glaze, but since I don't have spray equipment or room in my studio to store large buckets of glaze, I apply crystalline glazes by brush. Most of the time I mix a few hundred grams at a time, which is sufficient to glaze two or three small pots. Since the crystalline glaze con-

I use a portable flat lap machine fitted with diamond grinding and smoothing disks to even out and smooth the bottom of the foot with 100 and 260 grit disks. Since water is used in this process, I do this in the studio, but still wear eye protection. Self-adhesive diamond disks or silicon carbide disks can be attached to plastic bats and the potters wheel used to grind and smooth the bottoms.

WARNING

Proper eye and respiratory protection must be worn during this process. Do all grinding outside the studio, if possible.

tains no added clay to keep the glaze in suspension, you don't want to add just water to wet the glaze. To wet the glaze, I use a CMC gum solution by adding about two heaping tablespoons of CMC powder to one quart of hot water. I let the powder soak into the water for at least 24 hours. The soaked gum is then stirred, resulting in a thin honey consistency. I add this to the dry glaze, stir and pass through 40 mesh, then 80 mesh sieves. The wetted glaze should have the consistency of thick honey.

Apply the glaze fairly thick. I apply one coat by brush horizontally around the pot. When that dries, I apply a second coat vertically, then a third coat in a diagonal direction to the upper $^2/_3$ of the pot. Sometimes I'll apply a fourth coat to the top.

On the interior of vase/bottle forms and on the exterior of bowls, I use a cone 6 stoneware glaze. I selected a glaze that fits my clay body to create a watertight seal. With a crystalline glaze on just the interiors of bowls, I don't have be concerned with pedestals or catch plates.

Firing

Pots, with their pedestals and catch plates are loosely loaded in the kiln. In my 4 cubic-foot-kiln, I will have at the most a dozen pots. Avoid using too much kiln furniture. It takes more energy and time to heat and cool kiln furniture than it does the pots. Always use witness cones in every firing. Even if you fire with a programmable kiln and don't look at the cones during the firing, they will be the best record of the firing. Keep meticulous notes of every firing. Keep a logbook of your firings and cross-reference each glaze to its firing. Fara Shimbo and Jon Singer gave the best advice during a presentation at the Lattice Structures Crystalline Glaze Symposium in fall 2005: When you're testing, change only one thing at a time. If you alter the glaze in any way, change only one amount or material at a time. Do not change anything else. If you alter the firing schedule, do not change the glaze until you see what change the firing has made.

Should the pot come out of the firing with few or no crystals, take heart and give it another chance. If the glaze has not filled the catch plate, simply apply another coat of the same glaze or a different glaze and fire it again. Should the catch plate be filled with glaze, it will be necessary to remove the pot from the pedestal, grind the foot even and create another pedestal and catch plate. I have refired some pots up to five times before I achieved results that were to my satisfaction.

Cleanup

After the firing, knock the pedestal loose with a small chisel or screwdriver. Strike the pedestal material, not the joint between the pots and pedestal. I use a bench grinder fitted with a silicon carbide grinding wheel to remove any remaining pedestal material and glaze. I do all of my grinding outside and I always wear proper eye and respiratory protection. After coarse grinding, I use a portable flat lap fitted with diamond disks to even out and smooth the foot. Silicon carbide disks and diamond disks with self adhesive backing can be attached to plastic bats and used on the wheel to grind and smooth pot bottoms. Squirting or spraying with water while grinding will help keep down the dust.

Firing Schedule

Use one of the following firing schedules for cone 6 crystalline glazes. You will need to experiment to determine the best firing schedule for your kiln. The ability of the kiln to respond to rapid heating and cooling ramps is a critical factor in successful crystalline glazes. Kilns should be loaded loose, using as little kiln furniture as possible. Older, well-used elements may not be able to keep up with programmed demands of the kiln. I've found heavy duty elements begin to be unable to keep up with the programmed firing schedule after about forty crystalline firings.

Bottle, 7 inches in height, thrown B-Mix clay, with Fa's #5 (Revised) glaze with additions of 4% manganese dioxide and 1% cobalt carbonate.

For Manual Kilns with Infinite Control

- Low – ½ hour
- Medium – ½ hour
- High – cone 6 over
- Turn off kiln, cool to holding temperature (1850°F–1880°F)

- Turn on kiln to a medium setting and monitor closely.
- Try to maintain the holding temperature for 3–4 hours.

Each section of the kiln may need to have a different setting to maintain a constant temperature. For my kiln, a setting of #3 on the top and middle section, and "M" setting on the bottom section provided a fairly consistent reading.

For Programmable Kilns

Note: My kiln uses an "S" type platinum thermocouple with the thermocouple offset turned off. Each kiln may indicate a different temperature when cone 6 bends over. Use witness cones and closely monitor them until the correct peak temperature is determined.

- Increase temperature 350°F per hour to 700°F
- Increase temperature 750°F per hour to 2000°F
- Increase temperature 150°F per hour to 2210°F (this puts cone 6 over, cone 7 at 1 o'clock position)

- Hold at 2210°F for 10 minutes
- Cool down 750°F per hour to 2000°F, hold for 1 hour
- Cool down 750°F per hour to 1900°F, hold for 3 hours
- Kiln off, vent off, total firing 9–9½ hours

Higher holding temperatures results in fewer but larger crystals with more ground (areas without crystals) exposed.

Recipes

CRYSTALLINE BASE GLAZES

MFE (Dan Turnidge Revised)
Cone 6

Ferro Frit 3110.	50.0 %
Silica (325 mesh).	22.5
Zinc Oxide.	22.5
	95.0 %
Add: Lithium Carbonate.	1–5.0 %

Fa's Base (Revised)
Cone 6

Zinc Oxide.	25.0 %
Dolomite.	5.0
Ferro Frit 3110.	51.0
Silica (325 mesh).	19.0
	100.0 %
Add: Lithium Carbonate.	2–4.0%

Fa's #5 (Revised)
Cone 6

Zinc Oxide.	27.0 %
Talc.	5.0
Ferro Frit 3110.	50.0
Spodumene.	4.0
Silica (325 mesh).	14.0
	100.0 %
Add: Titanium Dioxide.	2.0 %

Colorants

Add the following colorants individually or in combination:

Cobalt Carbonate	0.25–3.0%
Copper Carbonate.	0.5–6.0%
Manganese Dioxide.	0.5–3.0%
Iron Oxide.	0.5–3.0%
Rutile	0.5–3.0%
Nickel Oxide	0.25–3.0%

Hunt Prothro
Surface Tension

by Susan Chappelear

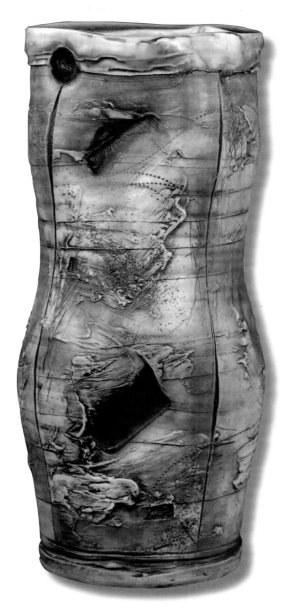

"Tahi vase," 15 inches in height, thrown porcelain with underglazes, stains and Gerstley borate wash, fired to cone 10.

When Hunt Prothro speaks about his work there seems to be a clear refrain: clay as metaphor. Color becomes a powerful symbol relating to human states such as tranquility and restlessness. The thrown form becomes subject matter, revealing emotional value as the gently swelling silhouettes suggest an abdomen, a navel. An expressive line encircles the curves and planes, leaving traces of a journey, just as a skier leaves tracks in the fresh snow.

After obtaining a B.A. in Theology and Literature, Prothro was introduced to pottery during the seventies through study with Marguerite Wildenhain at Pond Farm in Sonoma County, California. Prothro attests that the legacy of those summer workshops is a continuing presence in his life and in his work. Wildenhain was influential in mid-century ceramics and is widely regarded for the integrity of craftsmanship applied to utilitarian vessels and for her unique approach to teaching. She apprenticed at the Bauhaus in Germany with Gerhard Marcks and, in Bauhaus tradition, sought to erase the distinction between artist and craftsman that students may have accepted. Although Prothro rejects her absolutist teaching style, he describes her as having been personally enigmatic and he embraces her integration of life and work.

Seduced by early success in marketing thrown ware, Prothro contin-

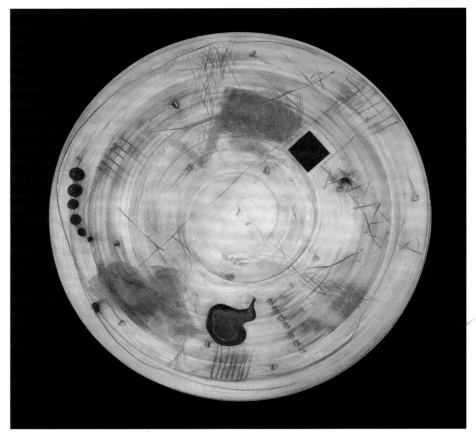

Right: Platter, 20 inches in diameter, porcelain with underglazes, stains and Gerstley borate wash, fired to cone 6.

ues to use a kick wheel to make a commodified art form. Using porcelain, he throws platters, bowls and cylinders in preparation for a cone 10 reduction firing with light reduction. He throws slowly and contemplatively, developing voluptuous shapes, which will become canvases for studied surface articulation. Referring to early Greek pottery, Prothro explained his preference for vessels with thick rims and shapes echoing the human figure. As a metaphor for the human longing for touch, his bowls invite handling. They are deceptively light, as the rims suggest a greater heft. Tension is heightened further by a subtle hesitation in the rim. Additional declarations of resolution are accomplished by melted fragments of Rolling Rock beer bottles residing in depressions within the rim. Glassy run-off occasionally occurs, merging with other directional paths created by incising.

Prefacing the demonstration of his techniques of developing surface tex-

"Blue Dot Bowl," 14 inches in diameter, thrown porcelain with underglazes and stains, fired to cone 10.

ture and coloration, Prothro reflected on his travels in to southwestern France to study Paleolithic cave sites. His impressions were documented in "Notes from the Paleolithic Project: Transience and Singularity," presented at the National Council on Education for the Ceramic Arts conference and again for the College Art Association in New York City. Prothro relishes the opportunity to consider the nature of human touch, the "pulse of the tool markings" and "the line that begins with authority but

ends in ambiguity" as ancient metaphors. He feels that the poetic, lyrical cave paintings he studied helped to inspire a more complex line in his own work.

And indeed in *The Mind in the Cave*, David Lewis-Williams writes about the neuropsychological percepts that structure such cave paintings, percepts that Prothro reproduces in his pottery. Dots, grids, zigzags and curves can be experienced without light by all human beings directly from the nervous system. By projecting these percepts onto a visual medium, an artist such as Prothro can reach back into history and reproduce the pre-iconic thought of Upper Paleolithic man. The caves of Lascaux blend these percepts with later-stage thought processes that produce and reproduce icons of that time, most obviously, but not limited to, the animal figures. In turn, modern man sees these animal figures as emblematic of Lascaux without quite noticing the percepts that adorn such figures. Prothro, however, foregrounds these linear percepts in his work, bringing history to his pieces by appropriating ancient artistic techniques.

With trimmed leather-hard bowls and jars of Velvet underglazes assembled on a classroom table, Prothro captured the audience as he proceeded to bring life and proportionate harmony to the ware. Using a porcupine quill, he created surface tension from linear movements over planes and curves, sometimes horizontally segmenting the cylinders into thirds with deep scarring. Defining planes with a canvas-wrapped paddle created subtle nuances of silhouette. Prothro says that the quality of line can become the content or "subject matter" of the vessel. We watched as a line bit, relaxed and faded into a mass of cross-hatched etching. An edge of a shell was rolled across the surface occasionally to add variety to line quality. Referring to the painter Paul Klee, Prothro moved from a bold, expressive line to deliberate, constructive hatch-

work produced by a wire brush.

During the gallery lecture Prothro drew a comparison of his early work to that of William Daley. He dismisses the "d" word, believing that the label "derivative" is unnecessarily feared, as art is imitation. Occupying one wall was a series of platters decorated primarily in a warm palette with notes of complementary color. His admiration for the American abstract painter Arshille Gorky is evidenced by the painterly passages of color and lyrical line. As in Gorky's canvases, the platters are intriguing, with spatial ambiguity marked by ethereal line. Chiaroscuro, which appears in the bowls as sharply defined, adjacent elliptical shapes of light and dark, is, however, more atmospheric in the platters. Accents of hard-edged shapes provide a focal point as they appear suspended in infinity. An oriental landscape can be imagined, or for some the platters may trigger a reference to Western action painting.

Other bowls and teapots on exhibit were decorated with deeply cut recesses. In these works, Prothro seems to be avoiding pattern, preferring to intuitively follow the shape of the pot. Another bowl, glazed with neutral color over a more regular arrangement of marks, suggests equilibrium by the even distribution of linear elements. In contrast, the platters and vases provide more tension and movement as space in some areas is so compressed that the eye is induced to follow an expressive directional line.

Round vase, 10 inches in height, thrown porcelain with underglazes, stains and Gerstley Borate wash, fired to cone 10, by Hunt Prothro.

When Prothro metaphorically speaks of the "bones of the piece" he is referring to life's physical urges and the dynamic implications of a work of art. Cause and effect are revealed as his touch pushes back again. Apart from connections we find to Paleolithic grid motifs or color passages and intuitive line from Abstract Expressionism, his sensuous vessels stir our feelings and we see forms whose parts are in a harmonious, balanced relationship with surface and structural qualities.

Top: Prothro brushes stains into incised textures before carefully wiping off the excess.

Bottom: Complimentary colors are sponged on to enliven the surface.

Mixing It Up

Although Prothro's underglazes are poured on a palette, he achieves all of the color mixing on the bisqued pot itself. He follows a sequence to keep all surfaces clean. He applies color to the foot, then the interior and, lastly, the exterior. The inside of the bowls are often painted in counterpoint to the exterior; related, but distinct. He says, "The rim is a third area, a point of transition, and a zone of change with all the attendant hesitations and gestures of finality."

He applies broad strokes of black stain to all sgraffit-toed surfaces, then gently wipes, leaving only the inlay to provide sharp contrast to the warm underglazes to follow. Without any masking, he carefully paints and dabs each piece to preserve a grid arrangement. In some of the pieces, figure and ground appear to be on the same plane, as hard-edged regions of color are jux-taposed to create contrasting tonal values and heighten each other's vital nature. This interplay of shapes and colors, which have no representational associations, take on a painterly quality. In other pieces, he achieves coloration by scumbling layers of translucent washes, some of which he spritzes with water to promote color bleeding and to suggest distant galaxies. He preserves the color effects with a thin, Gerstley borate-based clear glaze and strives to achieve a patina rather than a true glaze.

Kleckner Pottery
The Ripple Effect

by Judy Seckler

**Cups and saucers,
4 inches in height,
thrown porcelain
with applied slips and
glazes, fired to cone
10 in reduction.**

On a typical city street in Bethlehem, a city in eastern Pennsylvania, once known for its integral role in steel production, there is a converted brick warehouse. The two-story building serves as a studio and home for Jeffrey Kleckner of Kleckner Pottery. Inside, a showroom and an area for storing, mixing and throwing clay can be found on the ground floor. A gas kiln, a packing area and the one-bedroom apartment that Kleckner calls home, are located upstairs. The 3000-square-foot live/work space is part of his ongoing strategy to keep his expenses low while weathering the vicissitudes of being self employed.

What drew Kleckner to ceramics at the beginning was the studio potter lifestyle. From the beginning of his ceramics career, he was greatly attracted to the concept of producing work in a studio, just like his various teachers along the way. "I had this romantic idea," he says. He knew early on that he wasn't going to be a professional athlete or make his living sitting behind a desk. Instead, in high school, his fascination with the throwing process went hand in hand with the discovery that working with clay was rewarding and something he could succeed at. His high school also exposed him to a series of highly skilled visiting artists that gave added credibility to working with clay.

Kleckner went on to earn a B.F.A. at the Cleveland Institute of Art, where he studied under Joe Zeller and Paul Dresang. He learned the importance of making "strong work" from Zeller and began to think of pots as a vehicle for color, line, sur-

Jars, 3½ inches in height, thrown and faceted porcelain with applied slips and glazes, fired to cone 10 in reduction.

face, form and expression. Dresang, who is known for his trompe l'oeil sculptures that resemble leather objects, also contributed to his growing ceramics vocabulary. Of the many visiting artists that came to CIA, Warren MacKenzie, who studied with Bernard Leach, and Randy Johnson, known for his Asian–inspired pieces, provided lasting impressions for the beginner potter.

After school, Kleckner returned to Pennsylvania to work as a potter, but it took another sixteen years for his ideas about form and design

to coalesce into his artistic voice. The turning point came when he was working as a studio assistant to Dan Anderson, now professor emeritus at Southern Illinois University Edwardsville (SIUE). Anderson encouraged Kleckner to enroll in the three-year M.F.A. program at SIUE.

"I grew tremendously [during graduate school]," says Kleckner. The school welcomed many disciplines, and he was exposed to innovative drawing and painting. Beyond that, his work began to express more of his personal aesthetic.

**Box, 7 inches in height, handbuilt white stoneware, with
applied slips and glazes, fired to cone 10 in reduction.**

He still made functional ceramics, but now he found himself drawn more to changes in color, pattern and surface, and he placed more emphasis on creating complex three-dimensional forms.

These interests are demonstrated in something as simple as a cup and saucer. "I appreciate them as forms," he says. "How the pattern flows from the cup to the saucer." Each piece is wheel thrown and when the clay is still soft, he takes a wooden tool and pushes into it to flute the lips. Using the basic principles of color theory, he

chooses complementary colors for the inside and outside of his cups because of their tendency to "pop." The slips are poured into the cup's interior, and the cups are then dipped in the complimentary slip to achieve the exterior color and surface. For the dark green teacup, tiny white dots made of oxide combinations are applied with a brush. During the second firing, the dots grow five times in size, resembling glowing stars in the sky.

With his Asian–style mugs, he's involved in a different thought process. He starts with a rigid grid as his fundamental design form. The grid is brushed on with slip. Strategically dipped white glaze with a rivulet-like surface is applied before the second firing. "I try to play with opposites," he says. As a result, the color dances across the surface of the piece. It suggests a lightness while at the same time deconstructs the piece's mass. Kleckner's choice of colors borrows from Asian traditions, displaying an abundance of atmosphere and drama. Kleckner says that "the rich history and the complex process of ceramics" is what keeps him engaged in making pots.

"Gaining inspiration from myriad sources, including the wonderful Oribe pots of the sixteenth-century Japanese Mino period, Kleckner invariably seems to have a knack for finding quirky resources for his inventive pots," says Anderson. "Whether from history or nature, contemporary periodicals like *National Geographic*, *Smithsonian*, *Bon Appétit* or a kitchen appliance store, Kleckner is constantly and consistently rewarding the user/viewer."

When Kleckner throws his vertical

Covered jar, 7 inches in height, thrown and faceted porcelain with applied slips and glazes, fired to cone 10 in reduction, by Jeff Kleckner.

Application, Application, Application!

by Jeff Kleckner

In my mind, glazing is all about application: how you use your glazes to serve the identity of the objects you are making. It is not about having the ultimate glaze formulas, but more importantly, having the vision to be able to use your palette of glazes well.

I like to glaze, but it takes me forever: about four days for a small kiln load. To execute pattern and motif, I use slips on leather-hard clay, as well as oxide combinations on top of raw glaze; sometimes both on the same piece. Masking tape is often applied to bisque to control glaze application and produce defined edges between glazes. After applying glaze, the tape is removed and a cold wax resist is applied over the raw glazed area. Then the next glaze is applied and the application process continues.

pieces, the work becomes more architectural. Jaunty lids sit majestically on the tops of vessels, recalling pagoda roofs from ancient times. Part of the optical illusion of seemingly glued on mosaic tile is achieved by slicing off the sides of the stiff clay in vertical facets. The floating squares are drawn with slip when the work is leather hard. This technique has been one of Kleckner's most rewarding discoveries in his pursuit of complex pots.

Kleckner aims for luminosity aided by glazes that form rivulets or ripples of color. Similar to ripples that are formed when a stone is tossed into a stream or lake, Kleckner manipulates the glaze to create a surface tension that's easy on the eye and achieves a fluid spontaneity. Friend and fellow potter Terry Gess of Bakersville, North Carolina, says that Kleckner's use of glazes is tricky and has to be done very carefully. "When the kiln gets hotter, certain glazes run into one another but he is in control," Gess explains. "He has a very sophisticated sense of pattern and a subtle sense of color. Part of his sophistication is that he combines unexpected shapes, patterns, colors and motifs."

Kleckner maintains a rigorous production schedule in his studio, where he throws one day and finishes off work for two days. He keeps returning to the studio year after year simply because "the materials, kilns, firings and the rhythm of the studio have become a comfortable part of my life," he says.

Vase, 9½ inches in height, thrown and faceted porcelain, with applied slips and glazes, fired to cone 10 in reduction.

Recipes

Porcelain Body
Cone 10

Wollastonite	3	%
G200 Feldspar	10	
Kona F4 Feldspar	7	
C&C Ball Clay	15	
EPK Kaolin	15	
Pyrax	10	
6 Tile Kaolin	30	
Silica	10	
	100	%
Add: Bentonite	1	%

Willie Hillix
Cone 10

Whiting	21.0	%
Nepheline Syenite	43.0	
EPK Kaolin	12.0	
Silica	24.0	
	100.0	%
Add: Copper Carbonate	0.9	%
Copper Oxide	4.3	%
Bentonite	2.0	%

Val Cushing AA Revised
Cone 10

Dolomite	4.0	%
Whiting	33.0	
Cornwall Stone	48.0	
EPK Kaolin	15.0	
	100.0	%
Add: Bentonite	2.0	%
Titanium Dioxide	4.0	%

Val Cushing Base Slip
Cone 10

Kona F4 Feldspar	15.0	%
6 Tile Kaolin	10.0	
Grolleg Kaolin	30.0	
XX Sagger	30.0	
Silica	15.0	
	100.0	%
Add: Bentonite	2.0	%

Black

Add: Chrome Oxide	5.0	%
Cobalt Oxide	5.0	%
Red Iron Oxide	10.0	%
Manganese Dioxide	10.0	%
Gerstley Borate	10.0	%

Blue

Add: Cobalt Oxide	4.0	%

Mary Cay
A Glittering Obsession

by Sumi von Dassow

"Pod," 4 inches in height, porcelain, with Celadon glaze, and Celadon and red Glaze Kiln Jewels.

Many artists' greatest works have been the result of happy accidents leading to entirely new and unforeseen developments. Indeed, the ability to see the opportunity presented by an unexpected result and allow one's train of thought to be sidetracked onto an interesting and unplanned journey practically defines creativity.

Pottery, perhaps more than any other art form, is particularly subject to accidents, happy or otherwise. The alchemy of the fire and glaze leads to surprises, angst, joy and tears when kilns are opened. One small surprise is the jewel of glaze that occasionally appears on a kiln shelf under a too-heavily-glazed pot—most likely found in studios in which the inexperienced student layers many glazes. The pot that produced the jewel is usually a dud, but few could fail to feel a moment of delight at seeing a perfectly round jewel of glaze. Undoubtedly, many ceramics artists stash these little gifts of the kiln gods away to use some day, some way.

While a student at Metropolitan State College of Denver (MSCD),

Mary Cay became enamored with these little jewels and began collecting them during the kiln openings. Seeing myriad possibilities of working with glaze kiln jewels, she was determined to grow them—or as she quipped "cultivate them rather than mine them." The trials and errors of this project consumed two years of study, initiated conversations and recommendations from other artists, and eventually resulted in the

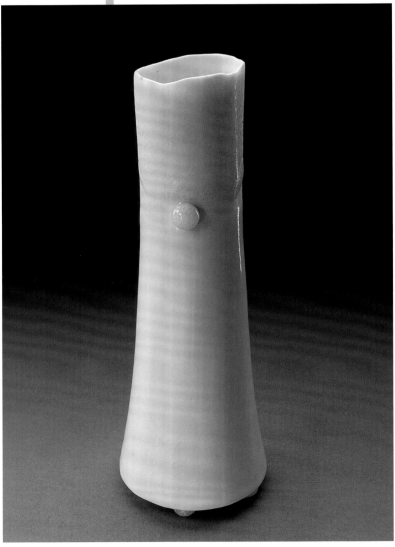

"Solitary Vessel," 6½ inches in height, porcelain, with Bone Ash and Sky Blue glazes, and Yellow Limestone Glaze Kiln Jewel.

project led me to use an element of scientific methodology by changing one variable at a time to achieve my goal."

Spending two years to perfect the manufacture of glaze kiln jewels may seem a risky enterprise with an uncertain payoff, particularly in a soundbite culture craving instant gratification. But consider that artists have consumed entire lifetimes seeking such elusive goals as the refinement of porcelain production in seventeenth- and eighteenth-century Europe; an investment of energy the legacy of which continues to this day. One can do worse than to follow the model of past masters, painstakingly documenting every success and failure, building on knowledge gained from successive firings, and developing an intimate and committed relationship with the work.

In the end, Cay found that the secret to making successful glaze kiln jewels lies first in taking copius notes and then in the proper preparation of the kiln shelf as well as of the glaze mixtures themselves. Different kiln washes are required for different glazes, and while some glazes work better if they are mixed with sodium silicate, other glazes work best when mixed normally, allowing them to settle and then decanting to remove the excess water from the surface. The basic method is to wipe a mullite kiln shelf with warm water to reduce its absorbency, apply a layer of a wax-resist and aluminum-hydrate mixture, and then apply two or more layers of kiln wash. The thickened

manufacture of thousands of glaze kiln jewels per kiln firing. The goal was reached, but equally importantly the process led to self-discovery. "Working with porcelain and glazes has taught me to be patient, reflective, and most importantly that timing is everything. Taking on this

"Planter and Tray with Pouring Vessel," 12 inches in height, porcelain,
with Bone Ash Glaze and Sky Blue Glaze Kiln Jewels.

glaze is then applied onto the damp kiln shelf in several rows of large drops using a syringe. After firing, the jewels are scraped off the shelf, washed and scrubbed on a piece of drywall screen to remove any kiln wash still adhering to the bottom. The correct preparation of the kiln shelf reduces the crusting making this last step as easy as possible.

Cay's technological achievement, far from being an end in itself, leads to numerous possibilities. On functional ware, a clear glaze is applied to the bottom of the jewel and after another firing becomes melded to the ware, making it food and dishwasher safe. When the jewels are placed on

Farming Kiln Jewels

Kiln Shelf Preparation

The first step in the process is to apply a wax-resist/alumina-hydrate mix to bare mullite kiln shelves. Mix equal parts wax resist and alumina hydrate by volume. Stir well and often. For Limestone Base Glaze, use four parts wax resist to one part alumina hydrate by volume. For Judy Cornell's Moon Celadon glaze, use two parts wax resist to one part alumina hydrate by volume.

After washing the kiln shelf with hot water, quickly apply the wax-resist/alumina-hydrate mix to the shelf with a sponge brush (purchased from any hardware store). Allow drying just to the point at which the wax is no longer tacky and then apply a second coat. For jewels larger than ½ inch in diameter or for the Celadon kiln jewels, apply a third coat. Note: If the wax dries too much, it will repel the next layer of kiln wash. To remedy this, apply hairspray that contains alcohol in even, sweeping coats to soften the wax.

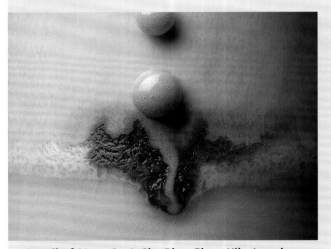

Detail of Mary Cay's Sky Blue Glaze Kiln Jewels, from "Three Vessels." The color is achieved by mixing Limestone Glaze with a strong cobalt glaze, but cobalt oxide or carbonate can be used as well.

Applying Kiln Wash

Mix the wash to the consistency of heavy whipping cream and apply at least two coats to kiln shelf that has been prepared with the wax-resist/alumina-hydrate mix above. For larger (more than ½ inch diameter) kiln jewels, apply additional coats. To make a smooth surface, spray the kiln wash with water from a spray bottle and allow to dry between coats.

Glaze Preparation

After mixing batches of the glazes, fill several plastic containers and allow them to sit uncovered overnight. The next day, decant all the water that is sitting on top and remix the glazes with a fork. Allow them to sit for another two or three days and decant again. The glazes should then be a very thick paste. Humidity clearly effects the decantation process. In Colorado, a semi-arid state, this process can be completed in three days.

For Judy Cornell's Moon Celadon, add 1 teaspoon of sodium silicate at a time, and remix to deflocculate the glaze just enough to hold a hemispherical shape as it is extruded from a syringe. For every 24 ounces of decanted glaze, 2 tablespoons of sodium silicate are usually added. For the Limestone Glaze, no sodium silicate is necessary.

Glaze Application

Apply the glazes to the prepared kiln shelves through a syringe and fire to Cone 10 in reduction. After firing, the kiln jewels will release from the shelves and can be washed off. If necessary, the bottom can be sanded with a drywall screen.

Post Firing

Kiln jewels can be refired onto ceramics using cone 017, 05 or 04 glazes as an adhesive, or attached with epoxy in a cold surface treatment.

"Three Vessels," 8 inches in height, porcelain, with Bone Ash and Sky Blue glazes, and Copper Sulfate and Sky Blue Glaze Kiln Jewels, by Mary Cay.

the bottom of a piece, they elevate the piece off the surface at the same time protecting the surface. On non-functional work (both ceramic pieces and mixed-media work) the jewels can be glued with epoxy or embedded in caulk. For bonsai-inspired planters the jewels rest on top of the soil allowing the water to evaporate less. In installations, jewels have been arranged on gallery walls by first gluing them to carpet brads, drilling $3/16$-inch holes in the walls and inserting the brads. Embedding the jewels in greenware and firing results in a finished piece oozing the sparkle peculiar to these gems. Cay's studio mate, Gail Fraiser, makes large sculptural vessels and has started purchasing jewels as embellishments to her Shino-glazed pots. Undoubtedly many new uses for the glaze kiln jewels remain to be discovered, a prospect which never would have materialized had the diligent investment in the process never been made.

Recipes

Kiln Wash for Limestone Glaze

Calcined Kaolin	50.0 %
Silica	50.0
	100.0 %

Kiln Wash for Judy Cornell's Moon Celadon

Alumina Hydrate	60.0 %
Calcined Kaolin	20.0
Kentucky Ball Clay	20.0
	100.0 %

The following recipes were given out during the summer session at New York State College of Ceramics at Alfred.

Limestone Glaze
Cone 10

Whiting	15.0 %
Custer Feldspar	49.0
Kaolin	13.0
Silica	23.0
	100.0 %
Add: Bentonite	2.0 %

Stains can be added to this glaze according to the manufacturer's recommendations. For Yellow Glaze Kiln Jewels, 3% Cerdec yellow stain was added.

Carbonates and oxides also have been added to this recipe with success by using various proportions. A strong cobalt glaze was mixed with this glaze to produce the Sky Blue Glaze Kiln Jewel, but cobalt carbonate or oxide also could be used.

A wash of copper sulfate can be sprayed or brushed on to create the Copper Sulfate Glaze Kiln Jewels.

Judy Cornell's Moon Celadon
Cone 10

Whiting	16.2 %
Kona F-4 Feldspar	50.5
Silica	33.3
	100.0 %
Add: Bentonite	1.0 %
Barnard Clay	5.5 %

This is a glaze that settles easily, so add 3 tablespoons of Magnesium Sulfate (Epsom's Salts) to a 10,000-gram batch of glaze.

Bone Ash Glaze
Cone 10

Bone Ash	5.0 %
Dolomite	30.0
Kona F4 Feldspar	40.0
EPK Kaolin	25.0
	100.0 %
Add: Bentonite	2.0 %

Knowledge in a Jar

by Morten Løbner Espersen

Installation of nine large jars at the Hillerød Public Library in Denmark.

I was commissioned to produce a series of jars by the Public Library in Hillerød, Denmark. I began this project as I always begin a new series of work; with a long sketching process on paper followed by clay and plaster sketches, carving and throwing scale models, and further drawings. To sketch more precisely, I made a scale model of the space, which is 230 feet long, 26 feet high and 20 feet wide. My aim was to monumentalize the installation as much as possible, to correspond with the surrounding architectural scale. I wanted to create a visually powerful series of works that wouldn't be overwhelmed by the enormous space, but at the same time respecting the character of the space.

In line with my earlier work, I chose to create a series of identically shaped jars, as I most often work in a series of pure and elemental geometric shapes. This allows the eye to relax in the repetition of the volumes, yet to focus on the differences within textures and colors. Jars like these are neutral archetypes, familiar shapes. They are not like the containers in which we store food or the ones from which we eat, but a container of knowledge—a jar that has always existed, in any culture, in any time. My ceramic forms must be honest and pure, being abstract vessels with no physical functional purpose, but at the same time they remain very real and present, and they expose the inherent beauty of the ceramic material. I wanted to make the installation as rational and simple as possible, and by focusing on one section of the long space, I intended the vessels to become more striking as a whole.

Large Vessels with Complex Surfaces

I formed a large foam block into a 1:1 scale model of the jar to make sure the size was right for the space. The model was enlarged 10% with a layer of plaster, to account for shrinkage. This layer was also useful in making a perfectly turned symmetrical piece. I then made a nine-piece mold of the form.

I used a 50/50 mix of grogged, iron rich clay and a neutral gray clay. I then added nylon fibers and even more grog. The clay was pressed evenly into the mold to a thickness of 1½ inches. Each of the jars required approximately 265 pounds of wet stoneware clay.

To ensure an open texture with a better grip for large amounts of glaze, the jars were covered with a heavily grogged slurry of the clay. They were then bisque fired to 1796°F.

All glazes were applied with a large brush. The inside was glazed once with each glaze. Then the outside was glazed with the same process, allowing each layer of glaze to dry before applying the next. I often started with a thick layer of Shino glaze and then added layers of colored glazes. On average, each jar had approximately 55 pounds of glaze.

"#1036," 35 inches in height, press-molded stoneware, with layered glazes, fired multiple times to cone 9.

Jars were glaze fired several times to 2300°F, adding glaze each time to build up the surface. Some were fired a final time with low-fire glazes or with lusters to an even lower temperature. Doing this preserves the structure built up by the stoneware glazes and lets me add bright, colorful jars to the series.

Initially, I was asked to create one or two jars that would be positioned at ground level. However, in analyzing the space I came to the conclusion that works positioned on the floor would be obtrusive and poorly lit, as the black floor would absorb the light. In the end, I chose to make nine jars, and to place them above ground, on a shelf that runs all the way through the space, 8 feet above the floor. All along this shelf there is a skylight. The direct natural light enhances the different textures and colors of the glazes, showing their richness to its full extent. Also, the position of the jars above head height requires the viewer to look up, and the fact that one cannot touch them may give the viewer an even more intense "tactile" experience through imagination.

When a visual language becomes too slick, it becomes dull, and when it is too gaudy, one tires of it quickly. In this series of works, I have allowed myself to try even that which I considered kitsch, such as lusters. While testing luscious earthenware glazes, I found that the juxtaposition of some "hysterical" colors next to subtle stoneware tones enhanced the strength of each individual jar. Employing this contrast, I discovered new aspects of ceramic materials. The fusion of shape, color, structure and surface, and how different glazes change an identical form, is always stunning.

The firing process can be a devastating force and I try to control its effects as much as possible through numerous series of tests. When working with layered glazes, even in a regulated electric kiln, I have to surrender to the forces and hazards of the melting process and accept the nature of the materials. I am thrilled and surprised by the violence they can contain. I often brush three or more different glazes over one another, although not too perfectly, as the unevenness adds character and depth. I also fire my work several times, adding new layers of glaze to achieve a more complex surface.

The Danish tradition of elemental, strong shapes and tactile glaze work has been an important starting point for me, and still remains an inspiration. At the turn of the 19th century, Thorvald Bindesbøll made remarkable pioneering work using the traditional earthenware with a restrained palette. He employed the techniques of skilled potters to throw for him. The Danish fascination for the modern vessel, and ceramics as nonfunctional pieces, started with him. Later, Axel Salto and Christian Poulsen broke new ground in two different directions. Salto made figures and expressionistic vessels with stunning, beautiful glazes. Poulsen's trademark was combining subtle, discrete shapes and rich, colorful stoneware glazes. To me, all three artists remain some of the most sublime makers in Danish ceramics history. I was schooled in Copenhagen and in Paris, where I gained a broad view on different ceramics traditions. The experience I gleaned in Paris has been of enormous importance for me. The French tradition is more flamboyant and extroverted than the

"#1033," 35 inches in height, press-molded stoneware, with layered glazes, fired multiple times to cone 9, by Morten Løbner Espersen.

Danish practice. I discovered that shape did not necessarily need to be constrained, but could be playful and even fun. This was liberating but also unfamiliar to me. I learned how to fix glazes that were not perfect (shiny and without cracks) and turned this information on its head, searching to get as much imperfection as possible into my glaze tests.

At the same time, I learned from Yoshimi Futamura, that the will and the forces of the clay were not to be seen as problems, but as the most important factors, which should be incorporated into one's work. One cannot, and should not, control clay and glaze fully.

Recipes

210 White Shino
Cone 9

Feldspar (Potassium)	40.0 %
Nepheline Syenite	40.0
Kaolin	20.0
	100.0 %
Add: Bentonite	1.0 %

215 Brown Shino
Cone 9

Whiting	5.0 %
Feldspar (Potassium)	12.0
Nepheline Syenite	72.0
Petalite	5.0
Kaolin	6.0
	100.0 %
Add: Ochre	18.0 %
Bentonite	2.0 %

300 Transparent
Cone 9

Whiting	23.0 %
Feldspar (Potassium)	14.0
Kaolin	20.0
Silica	43.0
	100.0 %
Add: Bentonite	1.0 %

307 Transparent
Cone 9

Barium Carbonate	30.0 %
Petalite	60.0
Kaolin	7.0
Silica	3.0
	100.0 %
Add: Bentonite	1.0 %

727 Matt
Cone 9

Talc	12.0 %
Whiting	23.0
Feldspar	23.0
Kaolin	32.0
Silica	10.0
	100.0 %
Add: Bentonite	1.0 %

135 Matt
Cone 9

Barium Carbonate	20.0 %
Feldspar (Potassium)	38.0
Nepheline Syenite	40.0
Kaolin	2.0
	100.0 %
Add: Bentonite	1.0 %

505 White
Cone 9

Titanium Dioxide	4.0 %
Whiting	4.0
Zinc Oxide	8.0
Feldspar (Potassium)	28.0
Nepheline Syenite	56.0
	100.0 %
Add: Bentonite	1.0 %

Tom and Elaine Coleman

by John Nance

In 1977, Tom Coleman was the subject of a book that told of his struggles to make a living for his family with his art. *The Mud-Pie Dilemma* covered his and wife Elaine's three-month-long preparation for a major show in Seattle. It recorded the high critical acclaim the show received and the depressingly low financial return—after expenses, they made less than $1500, roughly 65¢ an hour.

Tom, then 32 years old, already had a reputation as a thrower and decorator of classic porcelain forms. He considered the Seattle show the peak of his artistic work to that point and was sadly deflated by the sales. Elaine excelled in carving decorations, but was devoting most of her energy then to household concerns, the couples' two young sons, and the administrative side of the pottery business. Both remained determined to find a way to make pottery support their family.

Fifteen years later Tom said he expected the next change in his work "to make the transitions I normally make. I'll probably find new shapes and forms accidentally, the way I usually do; but with the acceptance of this work [at the Portland show], I'll be more confident to go in new directions."

Now, ten years after that interview and a quarter century after the struggles and disappointment chronicled in *The Mud-Pie Dilemma*, the Colemans have reached a new level of success and comfort with themselves and their work.

Tom's present work embodies major changes that are not as obvious as previous transitions. "Yes, I guess you could call this radically subtle now—ha! How do you like that? Well, that's what it is. If there's anything dramatic in what I'm doing differently, it's in my approach to color, to glazes; I'm painting with the colors, with the softness and tonality. Sometimes, I spray three, four, even five layers of glaze on a piece. But it still remains subtle."

He gestured toward a large platter hanging on a wall, and pointed to the softly burnished yellows and or-

Porcelain vase, 12 inches in height, thrown and altered, with Coleman B's Shino Glaze and dry mesquite ash, fired to cone 10 in reduction, by Tom Coleman.

Celadon-glazed bottles, to approximately 8 inches in height, thrown by Tom and carved by Elaine Coleman.

"Lizard Vase," 12 inches in height, porcelain with celadon glaze, thrown by Tom and carved by Elaine Coleman.

anges, browns and blues that fused lightly with one another at the edges of the different colors that spread over the surface. "These are all desert colors—come straight from the landscapes around here. And I'm combining them with all the old classic forms I used to throw. Yet there are elements of everything I've ever done in these recent pieces. I found that even the Japanese Shino glazes, with those subtle oranges and yellows, are very desertlike."

Coleman paused to think, then added, "A key point now is that I've learned how to put these wonderful colors on the high-fired porcelain I love to work with. Ten years ago, I had no idea how to do it. It has taken years to figure out—and color has been leading me."

Coleman found value in periodic visits to sites around Las Vegas, such as the Valley of Fire. "The color in the rock formations there is intriguing," he remarked. "I've been photographing there and elsewhere with my macro (close-up) lens, focusing in on rocks, plants, anything. I get so close that I don't see any shapes, just color and textures. And that is what I've learned to duplicate in glazes. It's exciting!"

The desert also caused Coleman to change his clay recipe to accommodate the drier, hotter climate. Most of his larger pieces cracked in the 100° heat. Now "the heat doesn't hurt the formula I've devised—in fact, it helps. I can throw or build something and it'll be dry enough to trim and finish that same day."

The finished teapot, 10½ inches in height, with celadon glaze, fired to cone 10 in reduction.

"Iris and Frog Plate," 14 inches in diameter, porcelain, with Dark Green Celadon Glaze, by Elaine Coleman.

Elaine's potmaking has become what they call "a total collaboration" with Tom. Formerly, she had made most of her own slab and handbuilt forms on which she incised decorations. But as she increased the amount of time spent with clay (now devoting at least one week of every four, or as many as five weeks in a row when preparing for a show), she stopped making pots and focused exclusively on incising pots made by Tom. She explained, "Tom is the best thrower I know, surely better than me. So why not do what I do best, carving the design."

Throwing with a rib on the inside also helps Tom remove excess moisture. "Removing the moisture strengthens the piece, makes a denser, more closed or compressed clay surface, so I can work it more. It's not a new thing—a lot of European throwers do it, and Americans have picked it up. Actually, I knew about it, but it felt uncomfortable. I was so used to using my fingers; I liked having the touch and feel of the clay, and thought I might lose something. But I tried the rib, got used to it, and now it's great—much better for Elaine's work."

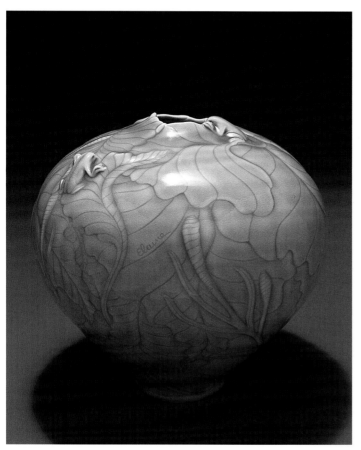

"Frog and Leaf Vase with Cut Top," 11 inches in height, celadon-glazed porcelain, thrown by Tom and carved by Elaine Coleman.

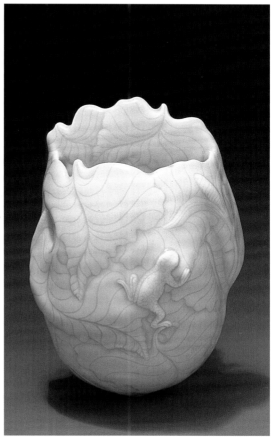

Carved porcelain wall pocket, 10 inches in height, with tin celadon glaze, by Elaine Coleman.

Elaine draws the design directly onto leather-hard pots with a No. 2 pencil. She studies the piece while rotating it slowly on a turntable, finds an idea, then swiftly, in a flowing series of seemingly continuous strokes, draws the design onto the clay. She then uses an array of needle-sharp dental tools and straight-edge commercial trimming tools to incise the design. Many of the images—a pair of lizards, for instance—are elaborate but with an artful simplicity in the way they fit a particular pot— harmonizing with it, becoming part of that specific shape.

She may sit before a piece for hours at a stretch, taking breaks to rest and massage her hand, as she goes over and over the penciled outline, carefully removing small curling strips of clay and smoothing the edges. "I go over each bit of a design at least three times with a wet sponge to smooth out the edges, make them rounded."

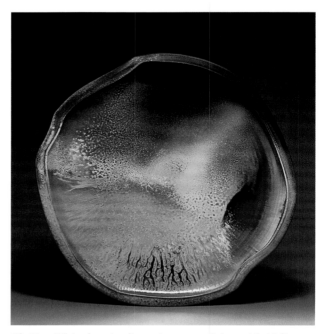

Platter, 23 inches in diameter, porcelain, with Yellow Crystal Matt and Black Barium Matt Glazes, with dry mesquite ash sprinkled on top, fired to cone 10 in reduction, by Tom Coleman.

Teapot, 10½ inches in height, with sprayed Patina Green Barium Matt Glaze and dry ash, by Tom Coleman.

Bourbon bowls, 4 inches in height, porcelain, with poured and sprayed Crab Claw Shino Glaze, and mesquite ash sprinkled over the surface, fired to cone 10 in reduction, by Tom Coleman.

Bottles and vase, to 11 inches in height, wheel-thrown porcelain, with Coleman Vegas Red Glaze, fired to cone 10 in reduction, by Tom Coleman.

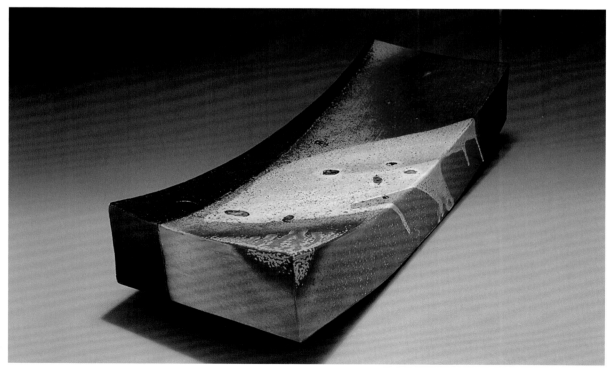

White stoneware table slab, 24 inches in length, with Shino and Barium Matt Glazes and dry mesquite ash, by Tom Coleman.

Recipes

Elaine's Celadon Base

Cone 8–11 reduction

Whiting	21.2 %
Zinc Oxide	2.7
Custer Feldspar	24.9
Ferro Frit 3110	8.8
EPK Kaolin	17.5
Silica (200-mesh)	24.9
	100.0 %

For white, add 0.7% tin oxide; for green, add 0.9% Mason stain 6201; and for iron blue, add 1.6% Mason stain 6391. Yields a smooth transparent glaze that is great over carved or incised decoration on porcelain.

Yellow Crystal Matt

Cone 8–11 reduction

Barium Carbonate	15.1 %
Gerstley Borate	7.0
Lithium Carbonate	4.6
Whiting	16.3
Zinc Oxide	0.6
Custer Feldspar	43.0
EPK Kaolin	13.4
	100.0 %
Add: Titanium Dioxide	16.3 %

For use on exterior or decorative surfaces. Yields a beautiful butter-smooth glaze that develops crystals. For a yellow gold, add 2.0% yellow iron oxide. Responsive to oxide oversprays. For a pumpkin orange, spray with Spotted Black Glaze.

Spotted Black

Cone 10 reduction

Whiting	6.1 %
Custer Feldspar	79.6
Silica	14.3
	100.0 %
Add: Yellow Iron Oxide	20.4 %

A satin matt dark maroon with silver spots. Works best as thin to medium application on porcelain. Can be sprayed or dipped.

Horsley's Satin Matt White

Cone 8–10 reduction

Whiting	26.0 %
Custer Feldspar	49.2
EPK Kaolin	3.2
Kentucky OM 4 Ball Clay	21.6
	100.0 %
Add: Titanium Oxide	4.9 %
Zinc Oxide	4.9 %
Zircopax Plus	13.0 %

A beautiful, creamy, smooth white. If dry mesquite ash is sprinkled on the surface, it will produce a textured butterscotch color.

Coleman Vegas Red

Cone 8–10 reduction

Barium Carbonate	2.5 %
Dolomite	5.6
Gerstley Borate	9.2
Whiting	8.7
Custer Feldspar	53.6
EPK Kaolin	2.5
Silica	17.9
	100.0 %
Add: Copper Carbonate	0.4 %
Tin Oxide	2.0 %
Titanium Dioxide	0.1 %
Yellow Iron Oxide	0.1 %
Zinc Oxide	1.0 %

Beautiful oxblood with purple undertones.

Barium Matt Base

Cone 10 reduction

Barium Carbonate	38.0 %
Custer Feldspar	52.0
EPK Kaolin	10.0
	100.0 %

For patina green, add 4% copper carbonate and 8% rutile; for black, add 6% Mason stain 6600. A smooth, buttery glaze that also works well with mesquite ash sprinkled over the surface. Can be dipped or sprayed. Intended for use on sculpture or nonfunctional surfaces; not food safe.

Coleman B's Shino

Cone 10 reduction

Soda Ash	7.0 %
Spodumene	25.0
Custer Feldspar	30.0
Nepheline Syenite	8.0
EPK Kaolin	5.0
Kentucky OM 4 Ball Clay	25.0
	100.0 %

For stiff surface glaze that traps carbon apply thick and start reduction around cone 013.

Coleman's Crab Claw Shino

Cone 10 reduction

Soda Ash	3.2 %
Spodumene	12.2
Custer Feldspar	8.6
Nepheline Syenite	36.0
EPK Kaolin	28.0
Kentucky OM 4 Ball Clay	12.0
	100.0 %

Yields bright orange color with thin to medium application on porcelain. Dip or spray.

Chun White

Cone 8–11 reduction

Whiting	16.7 %
Custer Feldspar	44.0
EPK Kaolin	11.3
Silica	28.0
	100.0 %
Add: Tin Oxide	2.1 %
Zinc Oxide	2.3 %

A bright and shiny opaque Chun-like glaze; great color response from slips and oxides.

Preparing Wood Ash for Glazes

by Kathy Chamberlin

Early in my career, I experimented with the use of ash in glazes and on surfaces to mimic some of the effects of wood firing in a high-fired gas kiln. Wood ash contains soda and potash, soluble alkaline compounds that can irritate or burn your skin, so I made considerable efforts to wash the ash to remove its caustic hazards.

At the time, I found I didn't have the patience, knowledge or resources for proper ash preparation. Recently, I started experimenting again with hardwood, softwood and vegetable ash, and I've developed a simple way to prepare ash for the glazing process. You can follow this method to prepare wood ash for your glazes and decoration.

Use ash in your glazes that call for wood ash or apply it over the top of a glaze surface immediately after glazing (while still damp). It is a good idea to test your ash glazes and application methods when using new batches of ash. There can be variations in the melting temperature and surface quality between different batches of ash depending on the type of wood or plant material, and where it came from.

The Five Steps to Clean Ash

Gather wood ash from a wood stove or fireplace (figure 1). Use a galvanized bucket for safety in case there are still hot embers. Be sure the ash is from a fire in which only wood has been burned, not trash.

Once the ash is totally cold, sieve and discard the remaining charcoal and wood debris (figure 2). Use a metal mesh strainer—a metal window screen works well—and collect the ash in an enamel or plastic bucket for rinsing with water.

Using a plastic or enamel bucket, rinse the sieved ash in water (figure 3). When adding water, the ash

Safety Tip

Protect your hands with plastic gloves. When beginning to rinse the ash, the liquid is very caustic and can burn your skin. Protect yourself against inhaling the ash dust by wearing a face mask or respirator.

solution shrinks and loses volume. I try to prepare a lot of ash at one time. Use large containers and try to do this step outside or in a garage where water is available.

Most of the ash will settle to the bottom of the containers (figure 4). The water is poured off and the ash is rinsed again, 3–4 times. Leave the ash to separate or settle itself from the water for a few days. The water

will evaporate or can be poured off leaving a solid mass of dry ash. To speed the drying process, spread the ash out on newsprint or cloth and place it in the sun.

Once the ash has dried, it needs final screening through a sieve (figure 5). I have found 80 mesh works best for me to prepare the ash for my use in and on glazes. Store the ash in covered containers until ready for use.

Spraying Wood Ash Glazes

by Mark Issenberg

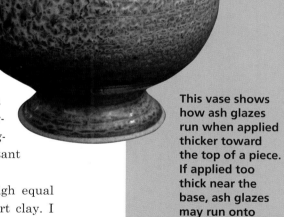

This vase shows how ash glazes run when applied thicker toward the top of a piece. If applied too thick near the base, ash glazes may run onto your kiln shelves.

I started using ash glazes because I liked the idea of utilizing a material that many would consider waste: wood ash from a fireplace. My original ash glaze was derived from a slip glaze that Leon Kula gave me, which was 60 parts Redart clay and 40 parts whiting. Although this was a very simple glaze, I wanted to use some ash.

While living in Miami after Hurricane Andrew in 1992, there was an abundance of wood for fires on cool nights, so I now had a source of ash and made glazes using 50 parts Redart and 50 parts ash. After moving to Rising Fawn, Georgia, the wood changed from mahogany to mostly hickory and oak, plus pine, walnut and the occasional unknown dead tree. From experimenting with different types of trees, I discovered that the clay made more of a difference than the type of ash being used. Through this experimentation, I also learned to use sprayers for applying an ash glaze.

To begin, prepare ashes by running them through a flour sifter to remove unburned wood, charcoal and big chunks of debris, then run the dry ash through a 40-mesh screen. I usually process a 5-gallon bucket of ash at one time. Caution: Wood ash is caustic, so work only in a well-ventilated area wearing a respirator, safety goggles and chemical-resistant gloves for protection.

The next step is to weigh equal amounts of ash and Redart clay. I only mix up what I'll use in one firing (1000 grams of each) since the ash glaze does not store well. After mixing with water, run the glaze through a 40-mesh screen then through an 80-mesh screen to get it to the right consistency for spraying. Use a thinner glaze than you would for dipping or pouring.

Due to space limitations, I spray outside, but if you spray inside, you'll need a spray booth with proper ventilation. I use a portable sprayer and set the compressor at 40 psi. I use a really heavy turntable that

A variety of spray guns and airbrushes are available. I typically use a variety of sprayers with different capabilities—some fill in big areas and others do thin lines.

Start at the top and work your way down, then return to the top area again to build up glaze. Apply a thicker coat of glaze only at the top because ash glazes run.

CAUTION

Always wear a respirator and eye protection when spraying glazes! Even outdoors!

Using a small airbrush sprayer allows you to do small bands and detail work. Note that the piece is sitting on top of an empty cat food can.

Recipes

Blue Ash
Cone 10

Ash	50.0 %
Plastic Vitrox (PV Clay)	50.0
	100.0 %
Add: Cobalt Carbonate	2.0 %

Light Green Ash
Cone 10

Ash	50.0 %
Plastic Vitrox (PV Clay)	50.0
	100.0 %
Add: Copper Carbonate	3.0 %

Angel Eyes
Cone 10

Whiting	20.0 %
Custer Feldspar	40.0
EPK Kaolin	10.0
Silica	30.0
	100.0 %
Add: Red Iron Oxide	4.0 %
Rutile	4.5 %

This glaze is originally from Jack Troy and does not run.

Oatmeal
Cone 10

Dolomite	20.7 %
Whiting	4.3
Custer Feldspar	53.3
EPK Kaolin	21.7
	100.0 %
Add: Zircopax	8.7 %
Tin Oxide	4.3 %
Yellow Ochre	2.2 %

Though not an ash glaze, this glaze does not run but works well when used in combination.

turns easily partly because I spray the shaft with lubricant each time I start the glazing process. You'll also need a gallon bucket with a small sponge for cleaning areas where you don't want glaze, and a towel to keep your hands dry.

With all bisqueware prepared and four to five sprayers ready to go, you can begin the glazing process. Start turning the turntable just before you start spraying. With bowls and platters, start with the bottom and glaze the footring first, then the outside body. Work with the spray gun about 5–12 inches from the surface and use steady even strokes to avoid getting excess glaze in any one spot where it can drip. Use a sponge to clean the footring. I don't use wax on bowls because the glaze builds up and runs off the wax, but I do wax flat bottoms. I then flip the bowl and spray the inside using a couple of different glazes. When fired, ash glazes run but some of the other glazes don't run at all. Testing determines how certain combinations will behave.

One of the most important steps to spraying is cleaning up the sprayers after use. Run lots of water through the parts of the sprayers, then set them on a metal rack to drip dry. Also drain the water out of the air compressor before storing it.

Wood Firing Clays, Slips and Glazes

by Sam Hoffman

Anagama-fired vase, 6 inches in height, wheel-thrown Helmer Porcelain, with pink flashing from Oribe Liner Glaze.

Since the beginning of ceramics history, wood has been used as fuel to fire pottery and sculpture. While providing the necessary heat to harden and vitrify clay, some wood-burning kilns leave dramatic fire marks on pieces in the path of the flame. Many contemporary artists pursue wood firing specifically for these richly flashed and ash-covered surfaces. As is the case with any artistic discipline, the process itself means nothing without a strong underlying form or concept of expression. However, when the technical and aesthetic considerations of wood firing are in balance, magical pieces can be born.

My experience in wood firing has been exclusively with anagamas. These single-chamber, tube-shaped kilns are designed to produce high temperatures for the maturation of stoneware and porcelain, while leaving the ware fully exposed to the direct blast of flame and ash. In an effort to emphasize the beautiful surfaces that are possible from such kilns, the work must be loaded in a manner that encourages good flame

movement and, consequently, nice flashing and ash deposits. When making work for an anagama, it is important to use clays, slips and glazes that are well suited.

When introduced to firing an anagama, potters often find themselves presented with certain "absolute truths." I had a particularly difficult time agreeing with two of these: first, that good anagama work must be fired very hot (i.e. higher than cone 10), and second, that work placed in the back of the kiln suffers because of cooler temperatures and less ash. While I loved the drippy, juicy pots that I saw coming from the front ranks of the anagamas, I also saw great potential for the quieter work that was in the back. Many potters like the idea of having a single miracle clay and glaze that works in any and every environment; this approach seemed quite limiting to me. Certain forms demand certain surfaces. I wanted to explore a variety of ceramic materials and develop several different possible approaches to wood firing.

I feel I have developed some exciting clay, slip and glaze recipes that are enhanced both by the intense blast of the firebox and by the quieter, more protected zones near the flue. I have had the opportunity to test these recipes in several anagama kilns and have seen a wide variety of surface effects.

Clay Bodies for Wood Firing

When I began formulating and testing clay bodies for the anagama, I was looking for workability, wide maturation range (cone 6–13) and nice surface properties (color, texture, ability to accept ash and flashing). I divided the tests into three groups—dark iron-bearing clays, light stonewares and porcelains. Several clay bodies in each category provide a nice palette with which to wood fire.

In the interest of lowering the melting temperature and increasing the glassiness of traditional high-fire clay bodies, I began introducing earthenware clays and soda feldspars into the formulas. After testing several bodies, I found that (in addition to lowering the vitrification temperature) the iron in the earthenware clay contributed to beautiful atmospheric and contact flashing. If carefully balanced with high-temperature clays and feldspar, any earthenware clay can be used in wood-fire

bodies. In addition to using native clay right out of the ground, my particular favorites are Yellow Banks 101 dark (not a true earthenware) and Cedar Heights Redart. Both can be fired relatively high, but also respond well to cooler wood firings.

I also found that by adding nepheline syenite to clay bodies, the ash and flashing patterns are greatly exaggerated, even in the back of the anagama. In proportions upwards of 25%, these clay bodies are essentially self-glazing. One word of warning about clays that contain nepheline syenite: they do not get better with age. Over time (8–12 months), such clays may become deflocculated because of the high sodium content, particularly if they were mixed with alkaline water. Wedging can turn these clays into gooey slip instead of causing them to dry out and become homogenous. When this happens, the best thing to do is put the clay back in the mixer and stiffen it up with more kaolin or ball clay. Another negative contribution of nepheline syenite is poor throwing quality. Most of these bodies tend to be quite short, which makes it difficult to throw large forms. After all, nepheline syenite is intended primarily for use in slips and glazes. After some practice, however, these bodies can be thrown into submission. For me, the surface qualities are worth the forming difficulties.

The clay recipes that I have included are the best that I have tested for wood firing. These bodies are all formulated for the back of an anagama.

Anagama-fired vase, 7 inches in height, wheel-thrown Flash 'N' Glass Porcelain, with Iron Slip brushed on exterior while throwing.

Using Commercial Clay Bodies

It is often the case that potters do not have access to a clay mixer or simply prefer to use premixed clay that is pugged and sold ready to use. The problem with such clays in wood firing is that they are often refined to the point of becoming lifeless. In the cooler zones of an anagama, premixed clays can look downright anemic, as if they were emerging from a bisque firing.

I have several recommendations for selecting an appropriate commercial clay body for use in the back of an anagama. First, select a mid-range clay body. Clay distributors often underrate the firing temperatures of their products as a safeguard. Although a clay body might be rated at cone 6, it can often be fired as hot as cone 12. Clay is most receptive to flames when it is at or slightly beyond vitrification. I have had particularly good results with clays described as Cone 6 porcelain. Several clay companies have actually started to sell bodies particularly designed for wood firing.

Another way to successfully use commercial bodies for wood firing is to blend two or more clays together. I particularly like the results of mixing terra cotta with porcelain. Grolleg kaolin, when mixed with Cedar Heights Redart, can produce phenomenal hues of pink, orange and red. Raku bodies frequently contain materials like petalite that are susceptible to flashing, and can be mixed with cone 6 porcelains with

This is not to say that they can not be fired in other locations in the kiln, or even in different types of wood kilns. In fact, some of my favorite wood-fired pieces are made from earthenware-based clays that were fired to cone 14. That being said, please test them before committing them to firebox temperatures.

good results. It is also fun to mix native clays, straight out of the ground, with more refined store-bought clay. Experiment with different additives, such as beach sand or granite, to develop textured surfaces.

An obvious solution to altering potentially boring clay bodies is to use slips or glazes to coat the surface. These can often enhance clays not designed for wood firing. Although the clay recipes that I have provided are intended to look their best when left bare, they are also well suited to taking slips or glazes for wood firing. These clays exaggerate the beautiful asymmetries of the flame path and tend to impart these qualities to slips and glazes that coat them. Conversely, clays that are too refractory tend to render uniform, unflashed surfaces, whether glazed or not.

Slips for Wood Firing

Slips for wood firing should be formulated according to the way they are to be applied. A thin wash of slip, whether sprayed, dipped or brushed, will tend to induce color and flashing while leaving the clay's surface texture basically unaltered. A thicker slip, however, will tend to conceal the underlying clay, allowing the character of the slip to dominate the piece. Slip also can be used for brushwork and textural decoration. Thicker slips are applied when the clay is still wet or leather hard, while washes and terra sigillatas can be used at the bone-dry stage. It is possible to apply slip to bisque-

Anagama-fired vase, 14 inches in height, wheel-thrown Laguna B-Mix, with Orange Shino Liner Glaze.

ware, but it should be quite thin to prevent flaking.

One nice quality about slips is their versatility. The slip recipes can be used on any clay body. While they are intended to enhance surfaces in the quieter parts of a wood kiln, these slips can be fired to any temperature. Again, it is important to test these slips on different clays in different kiln locations before committing any of them to important pieces.

81

Anagama-fired vase, 5 inches in height, wheel-thrown White Flashing Stoneware, with glaze drip from tatami brick kiln arch.

Glazes for Wood Firing

For the most part, I prefer not to glaze the exterior of pieces. I have found that simply lining pots with certain glazes produces a strong, vitrified interior to the vessel, and adds to exterior surface effects. Solubles, such as soda ash or pearl ash, and oxides, especially copper, can migrate through the walls of a piece and flash the exterior. Pieces lined with Shino glaze often exhibit glassiness or color where soda ash has come through to the exterior. Copper glazes can impart green, red or purple to the raw clay surface, depending on the amount of reduction.

The glazes I've included all have quite a wide firing range and tend to work both as liner glazes, as well as exterior glazes. One word of caution about wood firing glazes with copper; they tend to blush adjacent pieces with shades of pink. While many potters love this effect, some do not. Make sure artists with neighboring pieces are aware of the copper.

Although I am somewhat fanatic about testing new formulas in wood firing, never has a clay, slip or glaze recipe been the sole reason for the success of a work of art (although poor formulation can often ruin an otherwise successful piece). Without strong underlying form, surface effects are merely superficial. I have learned that there are no rules to wood firing, only guidelines. Use these recipes as a starting point and experiment with them. Don't forget: It is possible to challenge tradition while embracing it!

Recipes

IRON-BEARING CLAY BODIES

Dark Red Stoneware

Cone 6–14

Custer Feldspar	10.0 %
Cedar Heights Redart	35.0
Cedar Heights Stoneware	35.0
Kentucky OM 4 Ball Clay	20.0
	100.0 %

This is a reliable body with very good throwing properties. It can be fired to just about any temperature. In the back of the anagama, this clay was a rich brick red with mustard-yellow ash deposits. Small additions of sand (5–10%) make this body particularly well suited for throwing or handbuilding large forms.

Purple Earthenware

Cone 5–10

Custer Feldspar	10.0 %
Nepheline Syenite	15.0
Cedar Heights Goldart	20.0
Cedar Heights Redart	40.0
XX Saggar	15.0
	100.0 %

Be careful of how hot you fire this clay! It looks great in the back of the kiln and can go as hot as cone 10, depending on the form. The surface is a lustrous purple with black flashes and golden ash deposits. The fine particles of this clay body make it wonderful to throw.

Yellow Porcelain

Cone 8–14

G-200 Feldspar	25.0 %
Cedar Heights Redart	5.0
EPK Kaolin	25.0
Yellow Banks 101 (dark)	25.0
Silica	20.0
	100.0 %
Add: Bentonite	1.0%

This is a very interesting body. Depending on its location in the kiln, it can look totally different in the same firing. At cone 8 in the back of the kiln, it is a muted dark yellow with nice orange flashing and crystal growth. However, at cone 14 in the front of the kiln, it is a bright sunshine yellow with green ash deposits and purple flashing.

Anagama-fired vase, 3½ inches in height, wheel-thrown Soda-Fluxed Porcelain, with Navy Blue Terra Sigillata, by Sam Hoffman.

Recipes

LIGHT-COLORED STONEWARE CLAY BODIES

Speckled Stoneware

Cone 6–13

Nepheline Syenite	14.0 %
Cedar Heights Goldart	40.0
EPK Kaolin.	16.0
Tile 6.	27.0
Coarse Beach Sand	3.0
	100.0 %

This clay looks similar to Shigaraki clay, with bright orange flashing and small glassy burnouts of coarse material. It was inspired by Gail Nichols' soda-firing clay body and is one of the most dramatic clays I use. It is difficult to throw and trim because of the coarse sand, but the burnouts can be spectacular next to drippy ash deposits. (Some suppliers have beach sand.)

Gray Stoneware

Cone 8–14

Custer Feldspar	10.0 %
Cedar Heights Goldart	40.0
Cedar Heights Stoneware.	20.0
Kentucky OM 4 Ball Clay	30.0
	100.0 %

Gray is not often a color desired by wood firers, but I find it to be quite beautiful for certain forms. The surface of this clay can be quite dry in the back of the anagama, but also can have surprisingly nice flashing variations. If fired hotter than cone 10, it turns a beautiful golden brown with green and yellow ash runs. This is the best throwing clay body that I have tested to date.

White Flashing Stoneware

Cone 6–14

Nepheline Syenite	25.0 %
Cedar Heights Stoneware.	10.0
Coarse Fireclay	15.0
EPK Kaolin.	30.0
XX Saggar	20.0
	100.0 %

This is my all-time favorite clay body for wood firing. The surfaces range from delicate salmon and peach matt to bright fiery reds. It throws very nicely and can be fired anywhere throughout the kiln. If it is placed near the firebox, it has a tendency to trap carbon, which produces a beautiful range of blacks, grays and even purples.

Anagama-fired vase, 9 inches in height, wheel-thrown Speckled Stoneware, with Sam's Shino Liner, with "potters tear" drip from tatami brick kiln arch.

Recipes

PORCELAIN CLAY BODIES

Helmer Porcelain

Cone 8–14

G-200 Feldspar	25.0 %
Helmer Kaolin	50.0
XX Saggar	10.0
Silica	15.0
	100.0 %

Helmer kaolin is particularly well suited for wood firing. It has to be fired to at least cone 8 to avoid dry, melon-skin surfaces, but develops dramatic flashing patterns at higher temperatures. The smooth surface of this fine-grained clay turns a variety of colors, including orange, red, brown and yellow.

Soda-Fluxed Porcelain

Cone 6–14

Nepheline Syenite	24.0 %
Grolleg Kaolin	29.0
Tile 6	24.0
XX Saggar	14.0
Silica	9.0
	100.0 %
Add: Bentonite	1.0 %

This recipe was inspired by a clay body published in Jack Troy's Wood-Fired Stoneware and Porcelain. From cone 6–9 in the back of an anagama, it develops intensely flashed surfaces that reflect the flame path along the piece. Toward the front of the kiln, this clay is self glazing, producing glassy whites and oranges. It has a great tendency to trap carbon and can turn jet black if in contact with coals.

Flash 'N' Glass Porcelain

Cone 6–14

Custer Feldspar	10.0 %
Nepheline Syenite	15.0
Cedar Heights Redart	5.0
EPK Kaolin	25.0
XX Saggar	25.0
Silica	20.0
	100.0 %

In an effort to formulate a body that developed nice flashing and a glazed surface, I decided to include both potash and soda feldspars, as well as a little iron-bearing clay. The nepheline syenite lowers the temperature enough to make this clay look great in the back of wood kilns. The Custer feldspar encourages pinks, oranges and reds. This clay will usually be glassy if directly hit by flames.

PHOTOS: COURTNEY FRISSE

Anagama-fired vase, 10 inches in height, wheel-thrown Dark Red Stoneware, with Yellow Slip brushed on exterior while throwing.

Recipes

SLIPS FOR WOOD FIRING

Navy Blue Terra Sigillata

Cone 05–14

Soda Ash	2.0 %
Kentucky OM 4 Ball Clay	80.0
Water	18.0
	100.0 %
Add:Cobalt Carbonate	1.0 %
Manganese Dioxide	1.0 %
Red Iron Oxide	1.0 %

Mix the ball clay, water and soda ash, and let settle overnight. Siphon off the middle layer (the terra sigillata), then blunge in the colorants. Due to the small particle size, terra sigillatas are very susceptible to atmospheric flashing. This terra sigillata is mostly black, turning blue where it is directly hit by flame or ash. Bright blue is often not a color associated with anagama firing; however, this recipe can definitely be used to good effect.

Flashing Wash

Cone 6–14

Soda Ash	30.0 %
Earthenware, Ball Clay or Kaolin . .	70.0
	100.0 %

Mix and apply quite thin. Spray, dip or brush onto bone-dry ware or bisque. Try it with Cedar Heights Redart, EPK Kaolin, Helmer kaolin, Yellow Banks 101 dark, Newman Red or Ravenscrag slip clay.

Helmer Slip

Cone 8–14

Nepheline Syenite	20.0 %
Helmer Kaolin	70.0
XX Saggar	10.0
	100.0 %

Helmer kaolin has a tendency to flash orange or red in wood firings. Apply with any technique. It is rather dry at lower temperatures, but can develop beautiful matt surfaces. Above cone 10, it can be glassy and lustrous. Natural ash deposits greatly enhance this slip.

Yellow Slip

Cone 05–14

Gerstley Borate	13.0 %
Nepheline Syenite	12.0
EPK Kaolin	25.0
Kentucky OM 4 Ball Clay	25.0
Silica	25.0
	100.0 %

When applied thick on an iron-bearing clay, this slip turns a bright mustard yellow with white and purple flashing. On lighter clay bodies, it flashes orange and pink with touches of yellow. Since it begins to mature at temperatures as low as cone 05, it looks beautiful in any kiln zone. This slip also is enhanced by natural ash deposits.

Recipes

GLAZES FOR WOOD FIRING

Iron Slip
Cone 05–14

Red Iron Oxide.	25.0 %
Cedar Heights Redart.	75.0
	100.0 %

This slip is from David Leach for brushed decoration on porcelain. It can turn beautiful shades of purple and brown in an anagama. If applied too thick, it can have the appearance of burnt plastic. Natural ash tends to turn iron-saturated surfaces green or yellow.

Crackle Slip
Cone 6–14

Borax	5.0 %
Custer Feldspar	21.0
Calcined Kaolin	16.0
EPK Kaolin.	21.0
Kentucky Ball Clay (OM 4)	16.0
Silica	21.0
	100.0 %
Add: Zircopax	5.0 %

Apply to bone-dry ware or bisqueware to achieve the desired effect. Thickness is critical; too thin yields no crackle and too thick falls off the piece. The kaolin and opacifier encourage this slip to flash orange. Natural ash deposits flow between the crackle texture, yielding dramatic surfaces.

Orange Shino
Cone 8–10

Soda Ash.	4.0 %
Kona Feldspar	10.0
Nepheline Syenite	40.0
Spodumene.	16.0
Calcined Kaolin	10.0
Cedar Heights Redart.	5.0
EPK Kaolin.	15.0
	100.0 %

This is a great Shino for gas or wood firing. It is somewhat dry at Cone 6 and gets glassier the hotter it gets. No matter how thick this glaze is applied, it will not run. Wood ash tends to accumulate on top of the glaze, rather than melting into it, preserving the dramatic glaze drips that are often desired in anagama firing. The color varies from a light beige to a bright pumpkin orange.

Olsen Shino
Cone 10–14

Salt	2.9 %
Nepheline Syenite	77.6
EPK Kaolin.	14.6
Native Clay	
or Cedar Heights Redart . . .	4.9
	100.0 %
Add: Tin Oxide.	3.0 %

Fred Olsen presented this glaze recipe during a guest artist visit to Kent State University. This glaze likes to be fired as hot as possible. It is particularly beautiful if placed in close proximity to the coal bed, having a tendency to trap carbon and turn purple, pink or gray. It should not be applied too thick if placed in the back of the kiln, as it may shiver off of underfired clay bodies.

Recipes

Recipes

Malcolm Davis Carbon Trap Shino
Cone 8–14

Soda Ash	17.0 %
Kona F-4 Feldspar	10.0
Nepheline Syenite	41.0
EPK Kaolin	19.0
Kentucky OM 4 Ball Clay	13.0
	100.0 %

Use with caution in anagamas. If too much ash covers the surface, this glaze turns an unattractive, bubbly olive green. However, if protected by the ash and fired in heavy reduction, beautiful carbon trapping patterns can develop. Black carbon trapping can be resisted with wax brushed on just after glaze application. Great for saggar firing.

Helmer Shino
Cone 8–14

Soda Ash	10.0 %
Nepheline Syenite	40.0
Spodumene	20.0
Helmer Kaolin	30.0
	100.0 %

Depending on placement, glossy or matt orange with dramatic flashing. It traps carbon on rims or high points.

Sam's Shino
Cone 8–14

Salt	5.0 %
Soda Ash	5.0
Nepheline Syenite	40.0
Soda Feldspar	10.0
Spodumene	10.0
EPK Kaolin	10.0
Kentucky OM 4 Ball Clay	10.0
Cedar Heights Redart	10.0
	100.0 %

Favorite glaze as a liner or exterior surfaces. Combination of all good Shino recipes tested. Yields golden oranges to buttery yellows and often traps carbon. Wood ash tends to sit nicely on the surface.

Turquoise Oribe
Cone 8–14

Strontium Carbonate	9.0 %
Talc	4.0
Whiting	19.0
Custer Feldspar	28.0
EPK Kaolin	3.0
Silica	37.0
	100.0 %
Add: Copper Carbonate	6.0 %
Bentonite	2.0 %

This is quite unlike a traditional Japanese Oribe, but will turn a bright turquoise when fired hot enough. It looks best in a neutral to oxidized atmosphere, but will not turn red in light reduction. If applied to the outside of a piece, this glaze will flash pink onto neighboring work.

Leach's Limestone
Cone 8–14

Whiting	20.0 %
Custer Feldspar	27.0
EPK Kaolin	7.0
Kentucky OM 4 Ball Clay	14.0
Silica	32.0
	100.0 %

This is a predictable clear glaze that is an excellent liner if fired above cone 8. If used on the exterior of a piece, it must be fired in a saggar or it tends to shiver.

Paul McCoy
Layered Imagery

by Todd Turek

Paul McCoy, an artist and educator working extensively within the vessel tradition, has developed imagery that is both personal and expressive in an attempt to unite content and form. The ability of the vessel form to connect with the past and present, the agrarian and the industrial are among the ideas that McCoy strives to articulate in his work.

A member of the Baylor University art faculty for many years, McCoy has served, since 1996, as the curator of Baylor's Harding Black Ceramic Archive, which houses a large collection of the late San Antonio potter's works and his entire body of glaze research, considered by many to be the largest body of personal glaze study produced in the twentieth century.

McCoy uses a measured conservatism of form to provide formal support for his extensive layering of surface imagery through the use of paddling, internal and external altering, and the application of deflocculated slips. His intention is to charge his vessels with literal and implied references, which synthe-

size elements rooted in the natural world, industry, various avenues of human activity and his own personal experience. Recessed marks and raised patterns reminiscent of scarred trees, fault lines, tread imprints, and road configurations are often partially buried under dozens of layers of deflocculated slips. The resulting intensely textured surfaces, which McCoy effectively employs in the development of his "Urn" series often resemble the long-term accumulation of sacrificial materials on altar sculptures, and even the

"Testimonial Urn II," 18¾ inches in height, stoneware, with layered slips, salt fired to cone 8–10.

"Pampas Vase," 3½ inches in height, stoneware, with layered slips, wood fired to cone 12.

monolithic shape of these large jars echo the architectural complexes where sacrificial events occurred long ago. His decision to resolve the forms through wood- and salt-firing is McCoy's attempt to achieve one additional visual layer which supports and extends the underlying structures without obliterating crucial content.

McCoy's work also draws significantly from his life in the environs of central Texas, where the meandering Brazos and Bosque Rivers have created a subtle roll to the landscape and summers are characterized by a dense and often oppressive heat and humidity. Sometimes receiving very little rainfall, the vegetation becomes brown and brittle, and the earth becomes a cracked and parched carpet. McCoy effectively conveys his working environment through densely configured slipped surfaces that are often washed with iron stain prior to their exposure to the sodium vapor or the wood-fire fly ash of the firing process. Works

Details on Deflocculation

by Paul McCoy

The slip I use for building up and coloring the surfaces of my pieces is a deflocculated slip. The base slip is Robin Hopper's basic white slip, which is published in his book, *The Ceramic Spectrum*. This is the best general-duty slip I've worked with to date, adhering very well to any clay body I've ever used, even when applied very thickly. I deflocculate it through the addition of Glass Magic®, a sodium silicate in powdered form, which can be purchased at any major grocery store. It's used in dishwashers to eliminate spotting on glassware. Daniel Rhodes introduced me to this material and I prefer it to the liquid sodium silicates available through most ceramic suppliers. I add approximately one rounded tablespoon of Glass Magic to each 1000 grams of slip I'm mixing, dry mixing all materials (including the Glass Magic) prior to adding water very slowly, so as not to make the slip too thin. The slip is screened twice through a 60 mesh screen prior to use.

Because the slip is deflocculated, it dries very fast, even more quickly if a heat gun or blow drier is used, allowing me to add layers very rapidly until I achieve the depth of surface I desire. Also, if I'm using variously colored slips to emphasize the layers achieved in the surface, I'll slowly turn the wheel one way for the application of a given color, allow it to set for a few minutes, and then turn the wheel in the opposite direction for the application of a slip of a different color. Because it's deflocculated, each layer stands up well, allowing for the variously colored layers to remain visible.

For application, I've found that the inexpensive Chinese natural bristle brushes, which can be found in the painting department of any hardware or home improvement store, work the best, as the bristles are not too long and maintain a degree of stiffness, which facililtates the character of the application I'm trying to achieve.

To color the slips, I use 30% of any Cerdec body stain (manufactured by the Ferro company). Cerdec does make the inclusion stains and most of their colors hold their color very well all the way up to cone 10 in heavy reduction, although the colors will shift in salt- and wood-firing applications.

PHOTOS: BOB SMITH

"Pampas Vase," 23¾ inches in height, stoneware, with layered slips, salt fired to cone 8–10, by Paul McCoy.

emerging from the firings often resemble heat scarred surfaces, bringing to mind the Greek term for ceramics, "keramos," or "burnt stuff," a condition most certainly shared by McCoy after firing wood and salt kilns in summer heat.

The monolithic "Urn" series shares a geologic and human content with his intimately scaled teabowls. Although the two types of work address very different contextual histories of the vessel, both rely extensively on levels of surface manipulation, slip layering and the marks of the sodium vapor and wood-firing processes to charge the works with a dramatic visual weight. Alternating his work between the large-scaled urns and the much smaller teabowls provides McCoy with the opportunity to develop his visual vocabulary with a focused rigor. This work process, according to McCoy, "... extends my understanding of the range of intellectual and emotive possibilities inherent within the image. My primary objective is the integration of the forms' intended utilitarian function with visual and tactile information regarding the history of our collective human endeavor to understand life's greater mysteries, a visual record of the thermal forces within the firing process, and the eroding forces of nature."

Recipes

Hopper Slip
Cone 10

Potash Feldspar	5.0 %
Kentucky OM 4 Ball Clay	75.0
EPK Kaolin.	10.0
Silica (200 mesh).	10.0
	100.0 %

McCoy's Clay Body
Cone 10

Potash Spar.	10.0 %
Ball Clay	15.0
Grog	5.0
Missouri or Hawthorne Bond Fireclay . .	65.0
Silica	3.0
Mullite (40 mesh)	7.0
	100.0 %

Replacing Barium Carbonate

by Daniel Semler

Barium carbonate has long been used as an ingredient in high-fire glazes, sometimes conferring unique properties upon glazes. One of the alkaline earth carbonates, it has also been used as rat poison (large doses can be toxic to humans as well). Glazes containing it ought to be checked for barium leaching if they are intended to hold food or drink, or reserved for surfaces that do not come into contact with food. It is not my intent to present the research on barium toxicity here, but to present a course of action for replacing it in glazes.

Largely as a result of its toxicity, questions arise, from time to time, as to what might best be substituted for barium carbonate, and how much

should be used. Hot on the heels of such questions are those about how similar the glaze will be to the original. I wondered just how successful one could be in replacing barium carbonate in a glaze.

The usual replacement is strontium carbonate. Whiting is another candidate, because it is also an alkaline earth. The final alkaline earth choice is magnesium carbonate but it produces a more viscous melt and, in large quantities, promotes crawling. In this test series, I worked with strontium carbonate and whiting as substitutes.

I began with James Chappell's *The Potter's Complete Book of Clay and Glazes*, as well as various other recipe sources. I then went through them and gathered all the barium containing cone 10 glazes for which I already had, or could easily get, the materials. This gave me thirty-four glazes ranging from matts to satins to glosses, with a variety of colorants and varying amounts of barium carbonate.

The study consisted of mixing each one of these glazes in three forms, and then comparing the fired results. The first was the original, the second used strontium carbonate in place of the barium carbonate, and the third used whiting. All tests were done on Glacia Cone 10 porcelain from Clay Planet in Santa Clara, California. I mixed up each glaze and applied it to two tests pieces each, one for an oxidation firing, the other for reduction.

All substitutions were performed with glaze-calculation software. Substitutions were made on a molar basis so the ratios of total fluxes to alumina and silica were maintained (see "Molar Versus Weight Substitution" on page 75). In doing this, one finds that only 75% as much strontium carbonate, by weight, is required, and only 51% as much whiting.

All tests were fired in a downdraft gas kiln. I am very grateful to the kiln loaders and to Tammy Burwell who fired these pieces.

After firing all the tests, I finally had lots of information. The time had come to try to make sense of it! In order to establish some criteria for matching, I looked at the fired samples a number of times and made notes on each sample on its own and in comparison with the original barium containing glaze. In the end, I settled on five properties that are significant in comparing the glazes. These are gloss, color, fit, stiffness and feel. In general the stiffness, or degree to which the glaze moved, was the easiest property to duplicate in the substitution. Surface feel was the hardest, driven largely by the difference in feel between barium and strontium matts, the strontium being drier. There were a number of examples among the whiting substitutes that showed a greater tendency to run.

Finally, there is a set of glazes for which the whiting substitute produced a significantly, though not drastically, runnier glaze, than either the original or the strontium variant. This happens when the glaze is a matt or satin and the original glaze contains substantial quantities of barium carbonate and whiting to begin with.

These tests suggest the following, admittedly tentative, conclusions, though there are bound to be exceptions:

1. Less than about 0.2 molar equivalents of barium oxide appears to be readily substitutable.

2. Gloss glazes are easier to reproduce by substituting other alkaline earth carbonates for barium carbonate than matt glazes, even with relatively high concentrations of flux.

3. In matts where the matting is primarily driven by the flux, substitution is perhaps the least successful.

4. Glazes containing certain colorants are difficult to substitute with higher concentrations of flux, the classic being barium matt copper blue. Iron also can change color when barium is substituted.

5. The success of these substitutions was little affected by reduction versus oxidation atmospheres.

As always, this testing raises many questions. However, it does show that calcium and/or strontium are excellent, safe substitutes for barium in many glazes. Strontium does produce dryer matts and less dramatic copper blues. Calcium can make a glaze runnier, depending on the recipes. This knowledge should help artists looking for safer glaze ingredients for use in their studios.

Recipes

The poster-child for the difficulty in replacing barium carbonate in a glaze is SG-259, a silky matt barium copper blue. SG-259 is a fabulous glaze that is a completely different color when strontium carbonate (on the right) is used. The surface feel is very similar, perhaps a little smoother in the strontium glaze.

SG-259 Opaque Blue Matt with Barium

Cone 10

Barium Carbonate	38.4 %
Nepheline Syenite	48.0
Tennessee Ball Clay #10	6.1
Silica	7.5
	100.0 %
Add: Copper Carbonate	4.0 %
Bentonite	1.0 %

SG-259 Opaque Blue Matt with Strontium

Cone 10

Strontium Carbonate	31.9 %
Nepheline Syenite	53.1
Tennessee Ball Clay #10	6.7
Silica	8.3
	100.0 %
Add: Copper Carbonate	4.0 %
Bentonite	1.0 %

SG-259 Opaque Blue Matt with Whiting

Cone 10

Whiting	24.3 %
Nepheline Syenite	59.0
Tennessee Ball Clay #10	7.5
Silica	9.2
	100.0 %
Add: Copper Carbonate	4.0 %
Bentonite	1.0 %

Recipes

Celadons tended to show very slight color variation with the fluxes.
Racer Celadon 3, for example, is slightly greener in the strontium case.

Racer Celadon 3 with Barium

Cone 10

Barium Carbonate	6.6 %
Talc	3.5
Whiting	11.0
Custer Feldspar	22.1
Kona F4 Feldspar	21.9
Bentonite	2.2
Silica	32.6
	100.0 %
Add: Chrome	0.1 %
Yellow Iron	1.1 %

Barium Unity Formula

BaO	*0.13
CaO	*0.48
MgO	*0.11
K$_2$O	*0.14
Na$_2$O	*0.14
Al$_2$O$_3$	0.33
SiO$_2$	4.29

Racer Celadon 3 with Strontium

Cone 10

Strontium Carbonate	5.0 %
Talc	3.6
Whiting	11.2
Custer Feldspar	22.4
Kona F4 Feldspar	22.3
Bentonite	2.2
Silica	33.3
	100.0 %
Add: Chrome	0.1 %
Yellow Iron	1.1 %

Strontium Unity Formula

SrO	*0.13
CaO	*0.48
MgO	*0.11
K$_2$O	*0.14
Na$_2$O	*0.14
Al$_2$O$_3$	0.33
SiO$_2$	4.30

Racer Celadon 3 with Calcium

Cone 10

Whiting	14.9 %
Talc	3.6
Custer Feldspar	22.8
Kona F4 Feldspar	22.7
Bentonite	2.3
Silica	33.7
	100.0 %
Add: Chrome	0.1 %
Yellow Iron	1.1 %

Calcium Unity Formula

CaO	*0.61
MgO	*0.11
K$_2$O	*0.14
Na$_2$O	*0.14
Al$_2$O$_3$	0.33
SiO$_2$	4.30

* Oxide contributing to unity.

Molar Versus Weight Substitution

Let's consider two methods of material substitution in glazes. The first is by raw material weight and the second is molar (molecular) substitution. Substitution by weight is exactly what it sounds like; replace 25 grams of barium carbonate in a recipe with 25 grams of whiting. While this will produce a glaze that can be fired, it's likely that it will be runnier than the original. The reason is that 25 grams of whiting supplies far more molecules of flux than 25 grams of barium carbonate does. Substitution on a molar basis, on the other hand, will give a more comparable glaze. In this case, the total number of molecules of flux will remain the same relative to the alumina and silica. This is significant because glazes are formed by chemical reactions between the mol-ecules during the firing. The original recipe above contains 6.62% barium carbonate by weight, but the strontium version only has 5% strontium carbonate, and the calcium version only has 3.7% whiting by weight. Now look at the unity formulae; the portion of the fluxes that is substituted remains a steady 0.13. Thus, the number of molecules of each component in the fired glaze is more important than how much the raw materials weigh. Molar substitution does not guarantee that the glaze will be the same as the original, but the general degree of melting will be about the same in most cases. There are glaze books that explain how to calculate this process longhand, but molar substitution is readily accomplished with modern glaze software.

Recipes

In SG-266 we have an iron and rutile matt glaze. Here the match is in between. The color is not quite the same, and the surface texture is slightly off, the strontium being perhaps very slightly drier, though this could be application thickness as it's clearly important with this glaze. Some darker crystallization is noticeable in the whiting version. Strontium would appear to be the better substitute here, but more testing would be required to know for sure.

SG-266 Opaque Cordova-Brown Glaze

Cone 10

Barium Carbonate	23.6 %
Whiting	9.5
Custer Feldspar	56.0
Tennessee Ball Clay #10	10.9
	100.0 %
Add: Ultrox	8.8 %
Red Iron Oxide	4.5 %
Rutile	2.2 %
Bentonite	1.0 %

SG-266 Opaque Cordova-Brown with Strontium

Cone 10

Strontium Carbonate	18.8 %
Whiting	10.1
Custer Feldspar	59.6
Tennessee Ball Clay #10	11.6
	100.0 %
Add: Ultrox	8.8 %
Red Iron Oxide	4.5 %
Rutile	2.2 %
Bentonite	1.0 %

SG-266 Opaque Cordova-Brown with Whiting

Cone 10

Whiting	24.3 %
Custer Feldspar	63.4
Tennessee Ball Clay #10	12.3
	100.0 %
Add: Ultrox	8.8 %
Red Iron Oxide	4.5 %
Rutile	2.2 %
Bentonite	1.0 %

A Collaboration in Temmoku

by Joe Koons

Temmoku bowl, stoneware, with two layers of iron saturated glaze, a wash of Rhodes 32 White glaze, wax resist, gas fired to cone 11 in oxidation.

Sometimes we have no idea where a particular path might lead us, yet we are compelled to venture into the unknown, trusting that whatever we encounter will contribute something of lasting value to our lives. In 1971, my wife and I went to Daitokuji, Japan, to study art at a Zen monastery. We were able to travel to seven ancient kilns, including Seto, where we met the 14th-generation Raku master, Kato Takatoshi, also a master of the Temmoku Tea Ceremony. (The term "Temmoku," has its origins in China, and refers specifically to the shape of the stoneware bowl.)

In October of 1972, we took a second trip to Daitokuji for the Mushi Boshi: a de-airing and de-bugging of the works of art held at the temple complex. At this invitation-only event, we were allowed to hold one of the most favored bowls from Jian Yao, which had been used in a tea ceremony by Sen No Riku, the Zen tea master for the Momoyama emperor. My visits to Japan had a profound influence on my fascination with all things ceramic.

Red Temmoku bowl, 4 inches in diameter, stoneware, with two layers of iron saturated glaze, fired in an electric kiln to cone 11.

Temmoku

There is nothing new under the sun, and Temmoku glazes are no exception. It began with the discovery of black and brown glazes as long ago as the Tang (618–906) and Song (960–1279) dynasties of China. They can be seen in kitchenware of 100 years ago in Honan, China, as well as Japanese teawares and Chinese storage jars.

This type of natural, iron rich glaze is similar to those found in America, like Albany Slip in New York, the river-washed materials from Zanesville, Ohio, and glacier-ground clays from the Elsinore area of Southern California. There are many varieties of this type of glaze all around the world, which contain essentially the same components. They have a high silica content, which makes for a low fluidity at elevated temperatures and impedes them from running during firing.

My introduction to iron glaze-work began in the late 1960s, when my friend brought me a collection of teabowls that were produced in Jian Yao, in the Fujian Province of

China, during the Southern Song dynasty. In the '50s, James Caldwell, a Seventh Day Adventist missionary, and his whole congregation dug trenches at the site of discovery to excavate the bowls. Not only did he exhibit the bowls, Caldwell also conducted experiments, refiring some of the nearly 1000-year-old artifacts. He did the refiring work in Denver. Ironically, in later years when Caldwell was in financial straits, he attempted to sell the bowls to galleries and high-end department stores in New York City and throughout the country for the whopping price of $10 apiece. All of this is well documented in papers found in his Kansas City basement. Later, Caldwell's family had these "dirty brown bowls" that crazy grandpa had brought back from China, and they didn't have a clue what to do with them. My friend and I took the bowls to museums and dealers throughout America, and then to Japan.

In the United States, Temmoku is used to refer to glazes made from high concentrations of iron oxides. This is a misnomer. In China, the term Temmoku refers to the shape of the bowl made at Jian Yao. It is a cone-shaped bowl that, when turned upside down, represents a mythical mountain, a legendary mountain where the summit (foot of the bowl) can reflect the moon and the sun. It is the stuff of which Zen art is made. The artisans of Temmoku lived along the Mien River. This was a cosmopolitan, Zen–oriented center where humble and anonymous art-

Red Temmoku bowl, 7 inches in height, stoneware, with two layers of iron saturated glaze, fired with gas to cone 11 in oxidation.

ists worked magic in clay. Green tea flourished in this region and was traded throughout the world. The bowls went along for the ride. The bowls also were used as tribute to the Northern Imperial Court. In later years, even pirates coveted them. These artists and craftsmen founded the Southern Song dynasty.

James Marshall Plummer, in a 1937 London News article, explained that he first had difficulty establishing who had made these bowls and from whence they had come. The

Yellow Temmoku bowl, 4 inches in diameter, stoneware, with iron saturated glaze containing 10% yellow ocher, fired with gas to cone 11 in oxidation.

Japanese always called the bowls Temmoku for Tien Mu Shan, which means "Eye of Heaven Mountain" in Chinese. This led Plummer to explore the northern region of China where this mythical mountain was purported to exist. It was at the Tienmu Buddhist temple near Hangzhou that the bowl was first introduced to 12th-century Japanese visitors. Among its everyday uses, the bowl was used at the temple for wine. So naturally, Tienmu became the distribution center for the bowls and the green tea destined for Japan.

When Plummer showed the bowls to a local in the north, where he had expected to find the Temmoku kiln site, he was told that they were called Jian Yao. In Chinese, Yao means kiln site, and Jian is the area on the Mien River in the northern Fujian Province south of the Yangtze River. Plummer moved his search there and one day walked into the largest kiln waste area on the face of the earth. These bowls were merely kitchenware in the Song era, used for sipping wine or tea. They were the perfect vessel, nestling nicely into the user's palms. Five hundred years later, the bowls were elevated to the level of Zen art. In Japan, they were the culmination of simplicity and rustic beauty, perfect for the Zen tea ceremony.

Mixed Temmoku bowl, 4 inches in diameter, stoneware, with yellow iron saturated glaze, with overglaze of black iron saturated glaze, fired with gas to cone 11 in oxidation.

Collaboration and Results

Mel Jacobson and I embarked on this collaboration determined to learn the principles that produced these ancient glazes, to share the system that gives the best results and to dispel the rumors that have hovered about this art form for years. Typically, potters have to fire hundreds of pieces to achieve one rare work of art; however, we are able to reproduce our results at will.

We have achieved a richness of color that can be seen at varying depths all the way to the interface between the glaze and the clay. We have been excited to discover that, when you hold and turn some of the bowls, the colors change before your eyes. These spots change from yellow, green and blue to reveal an intricate system of satelite-like crystallization. Some crystals even reflect bright red.

We also have produced persimmon, lizard skin and even white temmoku. One particularly nice effect we are able to produce is a hare's fur pattern. Here it seems that the glazes boil and bring layers of iron rich glass up to the surface where they run down to a welt of glaze that forms teardrops on the outside, pooling into irridescent blue inside the bowl.

Chemistry

I have examined many formulas in order to determine what gives these glazes their unique depth. The recipes on come from the iron saturated glazes that Ralph Bacerra gave to his students at Otis Art Institute. In our research, Jacobson and I simply decided to fire these glazes at higher temperatures, and we found the glazes to our liking when fired in oxidation. Through tweaking the old formulas, we have arrived at glazes that flow sluggishly. Through bubbling and boiling, they show their character in thick layers.

The glaze formulas are mainly a combination of silica, alumina, calcium and alkali oxides. We are using potassium as the flux and calcium to assist in crystal growth during cooling. These glazes are not easy to melt or manipulate. Their high viscosity means we put them on very thick and then apply much stress through great heat—cone 11 and up. They are sluggish, but the imperfections flow and are then frozen in time.

To potassium feldspar, we add calcium carbonate and China clay in varying proportions in order to achieve a high silica level. Another important ingredient is bone ash. We also add red iron oxide and, at times, magnesium oxide and phosphorous oxide. These glazes have a silica to alumina ratio between 1:4 and 1:6, which is responsible for the low fluidity at elevated temperatures. The alkali (potassium) gives the glaze its brilliance. Ultimately, we are able to create the iron saturated glaze formulas that have their foundations in China's antiquity.

Temmoku Testing

by Mel Jacobson

Testing, for me, is firing an entire kiln load, never just test tiles. I have to put myself totally into the project and make hundreds of test pots. It has to be all or nothing. This was not going to be a part-time, test-a-few project.

In the summer of 2004, I had taken on a student/apprentice, Sarah Coffin. We digested all of Koons' written materials about Jian Yao ware, and read the history, as well as all the glaze chemistry.

We threw teabowls in sets of 60, each stamped with a new identity that would help us know how, and of what materials, each set were made. Each firing would be with a different clay body. We made hundreds of pots. We became ancient Chinese potters.

A dear friend, Susan Karrasch, studied Otto Heino's hare's fur glazes back in the 1960s while living in California. She fires a big commercial electric kiln, ideal for testing some of the glazes at Cone 11 with clear oxidation.

Koons sent me four of the old Jian Yao pieces: two teabowls, a dull brown bowl and a lovely small white-and-brown tortoise-shell piece. I spent many hours studying these pots with an eye for how they were glazed. It struck me that the Temmoku was dipped multiple times. It had to be. The roll of glaze at the bottom was multicolored, and it seemed that layering was the answer.

Knowing that the Jian Yao potters did not have the oxyprobes, refined chemicals, pyrometers and cones that we take for granted today, I knew I would have to count on my fingers the seconds each pot was in the glaze. I knew I had to make a hydrometer from a stick with a weight on the bottom, marked with a knife slash—simple things that an ancient Chinese potter would do. I had to glaze with layers, test many combinations and fire these pots to Cone 11 in a neutral atmosphere.

My instincts and experience paid off. The first firing gave us perfect oil-spot hare's fur and color we never believed was possible with Temmoku. In many ways, we are still in the first steps of testing this glaze/clay combination, but we can now repeat the colors and patterns we desire. We are actually making old Chinese pots.

We now understand the clay and glaze interface for this unique system to a degree. It is thrilling to use just iron in both the clay and glaze to achieve such a marvelous quality. As I have told many people asking after this study, this is not just a glaze recipe; it is a unique system of making pots. All of the steps must be carefully considered—clay body, glaze thickness, layering and very careful firing. It all counts in the end.

Small red Temmoku bowl, 4 inches in diameter, stoneware, with black Temmoku over red Temmoku, fired in an electric kiln to cone 11, by Mel Jacobson.

Recipes

Iron Saturate #1

Red Iron Oxide	8.0 %
Whiting (325 mesh)	16.0
Custer Feldspar	36.0
EPK Kaolin	16.0
Silica (200 mesh)	24.0
	100.0 %

Iron Saturate #2

Red Iron Oxide	11.0 %
Whiting (325 mesh)	15.0
Custer Feldspar	30.0
EPK Kaolin	8.0
Silica (200 mesh)	36.0
	100.0 %

Iron Saturate #3

Dolomite	4.5 %
Red Iron Oxide	9.1
Whiting (325 mesh)	5.5
Custer Feldspar	60.9
EPK Kaolin	4.5
Silica (200 mesh)	15.5
	100.0 %

Iron Saturate #4

Red Iron Oxide	10.0 %
Whiting (325 mesh)	17.0
Custer Feldspar	23.0
EPK Kaolin	25.0
Silica (200 mesh)	25.0
	100.0 %

Iron Saturate #5

Red Iron Oxide	9.4%
Whiting (325 mesh)	15.1
Custer Feldspar	40.3
EPK Kaolin	9.4
Kentucky OM 4 Ball Clay	5.6
Silica (200 mesh)	20.2
	100.0 %

Iron Saturate #6

Red Iron Oxide	19.0 %
Whiting (325 mesh)	12.0
Nepheline Syenite	21.0
EPK Kaolin	24.0
Silica (200 mesh)	24.0
	100.0 %

Iron Saturate #7

Red Iron Oxide	15.0 %
Whiting (325 mesh)	15.0
Nepheline Syenite	20.0
EPK Kaolin	25.0
Silica (200 mesh))	25.0
	100.0 %

Iron Saturate #8

Red Iron Oxide	14.0 %
Whiting (325 mesh)	19.0
Cornwall Stone	19.0
EPK Kaolin	24.0
Silica (200 mesh)	24.0
	100.0 %

Iron Saturate #9

Red Iron Oxide	13.0 %
Whiting (325 mesh)	21.0
Custer Feldspar	17.0
EPK Kaolin	28.0
Silica (200 mesh)	21.0
	100.0 %

Iron Saturate #10

Bone Ash	9.0 %
Red Iron Oxide	10.0
Talc	6.0
Whiting (325 mesh)	7.0
Custer Feldspar	42.0
EPK Kaolin	6.0
Silica (200 mesh)	20.0
	100.0 %

Iron Saturate #11

Borax	8.0 %
Red Iron Oxide	11.0
Titanium Oxide	4.0
Whiting (325 mesh)	15.0
Custer Feldspar	25.0
EPK Kaolin	5.0
Silica (200 mesh))	32.0
	100.0 %

Iron Saturate #12

Gerstley Borate	4.8 %
Red Iron Oxide	8.0
Rutile	7.2
Whiting (325 mesh)	19.2
Cornwall Stone	40.0
EPK Kaolin	10.4
Silica (200 mesh)	10.4
	100.0 %

Iron Saturate #13

Bone Ash	5.0 %
Red Iron Oxide	4.0
Rutile	9.0
Whiting (325 mesh)	18.0
Custer Feldspar	49.0
EPK Kaolin	15.0
	100.0 %
Add: Zinc Oxide	5.0 %

Iron Saturate #14

Red Iron Oxide	9.2 %
Whiting (325 mesh)	16.3
Custer Feldspar	42.8
EPK Kaolin	13.3
Silica (200 mesh)	18.4
	100.0 %
Add: Zinc Oxide	2.0 %

Iron Saturate #15

Gerstley Borate	11.0 %
Red Iron Oxide	9.0
Whiting (325 mesh)	5.0
Custer Feldspar	70.0
EPK Kaolin	4.0
Silica (200 mesh)	1.0
	100.0 %

Iron Saturate #16

Red Iron Oxide	9.0 %
Whiting (325 mesh)	6.0
Custer Feldspar	55.0
EPK Kaolin	5.0
Silica (200 mesh)	25.0
	100.0 %

Note: All of the recipes shown here were fired
to at least cone 11 in oxidation atmosphere

Many Faces of Iron

Marians

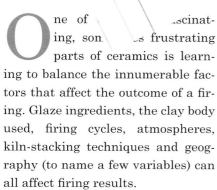

One of ...scinating, son... ...s frustrating parts of ceramics is learning to balance the innumerable factors that affect the outcome of a firing. Glaze ingredients, the clay body used, firing cycles, atmospheres, kiln-stacking techniques and geography (to name a few variables) can all affect firing results.

This may be frustrating if you don't control those variables, but if you do, there is opportunity for new discoveries. By changing just one variable, the same glaze recipe can be deliberately manipulated to yield different results. In this instance, I decided to investigate one variable in an iron-rich glaze: the cooling period.

I achieved greatly differing results in a single glaze with a single clay body, consistent glaze thickness and application, and the same heating schedule for all of the firings. The differences in the resulting appearance of the glaze on the pots came exclusively from their heat treatment after they reached maturity.

When the witness cone bends, the glaze should be fully vitrified. The kiln has reached temperature, but has not yet begun to cool. I studied what happens between that point and the return of the kiln to room temperature. I found that I could get a glossy black surface, a densely textured rough surface, a golden red/mud color, or anything in between, just from different cooling schedules.

How Does This Happen?

At the top of the firing cycle, the glaze is matured, but not watery; it doesn't flow off the pot. At this point, the glaze is not a homogenous melt, but a mixture of several melts. It is not fully blended. It may contain a dissolved second phase—in our case an iron compound—analogous to sugar dissolved in hot tea. More sugar dissolves in hot tea; less as the tea cools. The sugar precipitates as crystals as the tea cools. Our glaze, when melted, has a dissolved iron compound—the "sugar" in the tea. The iron precipitates as the glaze cools. So how does the iron form in the glaze?

Glaze is more complex and more viscous than tea, inhibiting motion. The iron crystals cannot precipitate and sink to the bottom of the glaze, nor can they grow very large, as the iron ions do not congregate in the same location. Instead, as the glaze cools, the dissolved iron separates out, forming numerous small crystals suspended in the glaze. The number of particles, and their eventual size, is affected by the surface texture of the underlying clay body, the cooling speed of the melt, the thickness of the glaze application and several other factors. The competition between the number and size of particles as the glaze cools results in the variety of desirable effects (see accompanying figures).

As it cools, the glaze becomes progressively more viscous and less mobile, until it reaches a temperature at which it "freezes" and nothing can move or precipitate within it. If the glaze is held at a temperature high enough to permit continued mobility of the iron into progressively larger crystals, but low enough that the glaze doesn't run off the pot, the surface will become matt. The multitude of tiny iron particles disrupt light transmission. Otherwise, the glaze solidifies with the same smooth, glossy surface as it had while fully melted. If the glaze is cooled quickly, few visible, very small particles form. Most of the visible color is the reflection off the smooth surface. This gives an aesthetically pleasing clear glossy black glaze, somewhat akin to a temmoku (see test 1). The opacity and depth of the glossy black show that the glaze can dissolve quite a lot of iron.

As the glaze cools and becomes more viscous, crystals begin to form at edges and imperfections in the body. If the glaze layer is thin, different kinds and shapes of crystal will form. If the crystals are stuck to the clay body at the bottom of a thick opaque glaze layer, they will be largely invisible. Crystals that float on top of the glaze give the appearance of sandpaper, which can present utilitarian problems. We want the crystals near the surface but not on it, large enough to create surface and color effects, but not be overwhelming.

A series of cool-down profiles with lots of jigs and jags showcases a different phase, exposing a range of surface effects. This translates into profiles with one or more narrow temperature ranges with extreme slow cooling and/or long holds, and possibly no retarded cooling outside the selected ranges. Since extended firing cycles can be costly, I framed my experiments with a maximum extension to the firing cycle of four hours.

I started out with the firing profile in Hesselberth and Roy's *Mastering Cone 6 Glazes*. The ramp for reaching temperature was a fast rise (200°F in the first hour, then 500°F per hour to 2100°F) until the last three hours, which had a rise of approximately 30°F per hour. Orton cones showed a hard cone 6. These firings were done in a very old Skutt 1227 with a computer controller. I examined the results of my firings and based my next firings on those

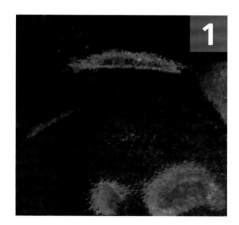

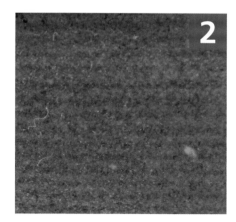

results, only changing one factor with each firing. I chose 1450°F as a low end for controlled cooling, selecting intervals for markedly slow cooling in the 2200°–1450°F range.

Speculation

With this limited series of tests, I produced a variety of textures and colors, by "poking" the cool-down profile. Each firing included several identically glazed test pieces distributed throughout the kiln. I obtained an encouraging indication that the different results were caused by the cooling-down profiles and not extraneous effects. I next will explore whether maximal particle size growth takes place "hotter" than the temperature at which the greatest number of particles is formed. Cooling to approximately 1600°F, then reheating to around 1800°F should obtain both good numbers and development of microcrystals.

Test 1

Cool down: A continuous cool from cone 6 to 1500°F at −150° per hour.

Results: This is the cool-down profile from Hesselberth and Roy. It gave a predominantly glossy black glaze, not greatly different from the quick cool, but with a hint of variegated color. I could see isolated metallic bronze and red flecks, but no crystals breaking the surface.

Test 2

Cool down: An uncontrolled drop from 2200°F to 1750°F, then −50° per hour from 1750°F to 1500°F.

Results: The cooling was slower from 2200°F down to 1450°F. Because the solubility of iron in glaze decreases at lower temperatures, I cooled at $1/3$ the speed between 1750°F and 1500°F. The result was a substantially textured surface, with much visible variation, and crystals of a variety of colors breaking the surface. The glossy black was gone, and the surface variation uniformly distributed. There were a relatively small number of largish particles. The color was intermixed red, bronze and mud brown. Bronze predominated where the glaze was thickest. I interpreted this as substantial particle growth below 1750°F, with little precipitation of new particles.

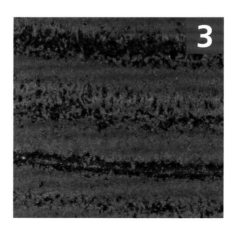

Test 3

Cool down: An uncontrolled drop to 1750°F, then −50° per hour to 1600°F, a hold at 1600°F for one hour, then −50° per hour to 1500°F.

Results: By adding a one-hour hold at 1600°F, the color shifted from gold/brown to red/gold. The red and brown regions followed the throwing lines, indicating that glaze thickness has significant influence. The strength of this effect showed there is a critical region for this glaze's development somewhere near the temperature 1600°F.

Test 4

Cool down: An uncontrolled drop to 1750°F, hold at 1750°F for half an hour, then −50° per hour to 1650°F, hold at 1650°F for one hour, then −50° per hour to 1500°F.

Results: Adding a half-hour hold at 1750°F and a one-hour hold at 1650°F gave smaller particles and a near-smooth, lustrous satin, variegated bronze glaze with small specks of red and brown. The original glossy black was completely gone. Color variation in the throw-

ing line showed the considerable effect that glaze thickness has. The half-hour hold at 1750°F facilitated the formation of a large number of small particles, leaving little free iron to add to crystal growth later. This uniform result was much like a pointillist painting, with exceedingly fine points. Moving the hold from 1600°F up to 1650°F could have a similar effect. Alternatively, we could see this change as a result of the glaze spending more time in the critical temperature interval for crystal development.

Test 5

Cool down: An uncontrolled drop to 1800°F, then −50° per hour to 1450°F.

Results: As the previous test result could have come from extended time in the crystal growing range, or specifically from the hold at 1650°F and 1750°F, I gave this firing just as much time in the sensitive zone, but uniform decrease in temperature over the extended region. The results were similar to the previous test, but with larger grain size and

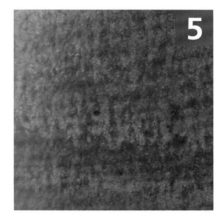

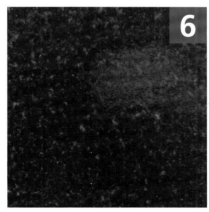

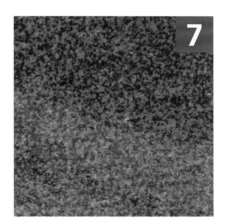

a lizard-skin feel to the texture. The glaze was mottled and less uniform. The smooth satin look was gone. I concluded one of the holds in the previous test hit the "sweet spot," at which point many small particles form. I did not know at which level.

Test 6

Cool down: An uncontrolled drop to 2000°F, then −50° per hour to 1650°F.

Results: The slow cool from 2000°F to 1650°F gave a surface and color as in test 1, with a much greater number of gold particles. This also shows that the effects of test 4 depended on the 1650°F hold. This critical test showed that the greater color effect I wanted needed two holds.

Test 7

Cool down: From cone 6 to 2100°F at −50° per hour, then uncontrolled cooling to 1700°F, then −25° per hour to 1600°F.

Results: To test a second slow-cooling region, the kiln was cooled quickly from a peak of 1700°F, then slowly to 1600°F. The result was an

intensely variegated effect with relatively few but larger particles in red and brown. The throwing lines were not prominent, so glaze thickness was not as important. The texture is lizard-skin satin, not the gloss of tests 1 and 5, nor the smooth satin of test 4. This result was related, but not quite like anything previous. This could be a jumping off point for a new series of tests.

Recipes

The glaze used in these tests is a minor modification of the glaze GA16 from Michael Bailey's *Cone 6 Glazes*, poured thick on Georgies Ceramic Supply's G Mix 6 clay body.

GA16 Variation

Cone 6

Bone Ash	4.6 %
Dolomite	13.6
Lithium Carbonate	4.6
Red Iron Oxide	9.1
Unispar	22.7
Bentonite	1.8
Kentucky OM 4 Ball Clay	20.9
Silica	22.7
	100.0 %

Empirical Formula

CaO	0.4126
K_2O	0.0454
Li_2O	0.2013
MgO	0.2521
Na_2O	0.0886
Al_2O_3	0.3424
SiO_2	2.7566
P_2O_5	0.0480
Fe_2O_3	0.1912
TiO_2	0.0104

Expand Your Glaze Palette

by Lou Roess

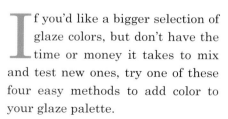

If you'd like a bigger selection of glaze colors, but don't have the time or money it takes to mix and test new ones, try one of these four easy methods to add color to your glaze palette.

Method 1

The quickest way to get more colors is to make half-and-half mixes of your current glazes. Combining ¼ cup each of any two glazes will give you enough glaze to cover a test tile, small plate or bowl. Just one example: Mixing a dark glaze half-and-half with a white one gives you a lighter version (figures 1–3).

Now, try it yourself. Six- or eight-ounce yogurt cups make handy containers. Mark the glaze combinations on both the cup and the lid. You can speed up labeling by numbering your glazes so you don't have to write out the full name. After firing, you'll discover some combinations you like.

Doing a line blend is a good way to see how intermediate colors will look (figure 4). Combine two glazes together in two different amounts. Incrementally increasing the amount of one glaze and decreasing the amount of the other for each segment can produce many variations. Note that most of the change takes place on the right side of the plate. This indicates that after a point the darker color overtook the lighter one. A light version of this combination could be used on the body of a bowl with a darker version on the rim to add interest. Now, try mixing equal parts of three different glazes to discover even more glaze possibilities.

112

Roll out a slab of clay and divide into 1-inch squares. (from left to right) Mark a design in each square. Glaze each 1-inch horizontal strip with a different glaze. Repeat the same sequence of glazes vertically. Fire the grid to see how each glaze looks both over and under all the other glazes.

Method 2

Another way to get more colors is to apply different glazes over or under one another. The best way to check out how your glazes will look when applied this way is to make a test grid. Roll out a fairly thick slab of clay, allowing 1 inch each in depth and width for each glaze you want to test. For example, if you have eight glazes, make your grid 8×8 inches. Now, measure out a row with a 1-inch-wide ruler, rolling the edge of the ruler onto the clay to make a line. Repeat for the next row and so on. Make the columns in the same way.

Next, use a stamp to make a design in each individual square or drag a small fork in a wavy line across the width of each 1-inch square. After firing, this will show you how the glaze breaks (figure 5). Mark out an equivalent grid on paper to record your entries; it doesn't have to be to scale.

Bisque your clay slab. (If you're using paper clay you can usually get away with once firing.) Begin by brushing your first glaze in a horizontal line from left to right across the top 1-inch stripe of the grid. Record this glaze on your paper grid. If you make the first stripe a white glaze you will have a good idea of how the other glazes will look over white clay. Brush the second glaze across the next horizontal stripe and record it on your paper grid. Continue brushing different glazes, one to each grid stripe, until all the horizontal stripes are covered.

When the last glaze is no longer wet looking, start on the left and add vertical stripes in the same order you applied the horizontal stripes. For example, if you started with white horizontally, start with white vertically. Brush the second glaze vertically in the next column, and so on, until you've applied all the glazes (figure 6). Make sure to record your glazes on the paper grid.

Fire the grid and mount it on a piece of cardboard. It's a good idea to

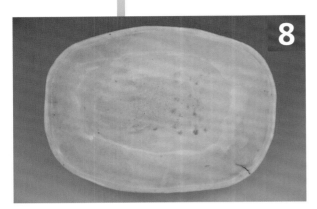

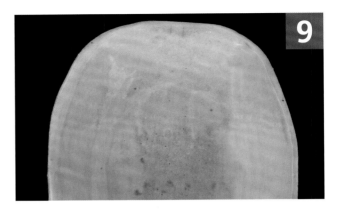

Distribute a pinch of oxide evenly to your glaze. Apply the glaze by dabbing with a sponge. The base color will look speckled after firing.

write the glazes in the order used on the back of the cardboard, then attach the finished grid to your studio wall so it's handy for reference.

You will now have a good idea of how each glaze looks both over and under all the other glazes. The vertical stripes will be "over" and the horizontal stripes "under" (figure 7). While this flat method doesn't tell you how the glazes move on a vertical surface, it does uncover colors of interest which you can test further.

Apply varying thicknesses of the same glaze to achieve subtle differences.

Method 3

A third way to get a new look from your glazes involves a base glaze with a small amount of coloring oxides (especially cobalt oxide, which is notable for being hard to combine in a glaze) distributed evenly in it. Stir thoroughly, but don't blunge or sieve.

Pour or dab it on with a sponge (figure 8). If you brush the glaze on or dip it, you're apt to get streaks. A white base works well with this method. You may want to apply a first coat of the glaze without speckles for better coverage. The fired result is usually a mottled finish with some speckles of oxide (figure 9).

Method 4

Another easy way to add to your color palette is by varying your application. You can often get subtle but noticeable differences in color by applying glazes in varying thicknesses (figure 10).

Using some or all of these simple methods, you can easily add variety and interest to your glaze palette.

Glazing for Success

by Annie Chrietzberg

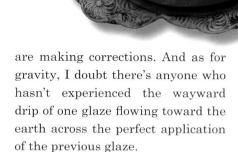

"Auntie Myrtle: A Covered Dish." Glazing complicated pieces requires pouring, dipping and brushing of glazes. Practicing with various techniques ensures greater success with each piece you complete.

Glazing, for a lot of people, is the bane of their ceramic lives. While there's no specific glazing system that fits everyone's needs and preferences, the more information you have allows you more options when you get into a glazing corner. My system for glazing evolved with my own body of work, and as the work changes, I draw on various aspects of it to suit the particulars of the pieces in front of me.

For complex forms consisting of thrown and textured elements, I use a combination of pouring, dipping and brushing to get the color where I want it. Dipping is the easiest way to ensure an even application, and pouring, with a little practice, is the next. Brushing takes more practice, time and attention, and I only use it when the first two methods are not options for a tricky place on a pot.

The two troublemakers involved with glaze application are water and gravity. When a bisque pot becomes too saturated with water, it won't accept glaze correctly, so use the least amount of water possible when glazing, including when you are making corrections. And as for gravity, I doubt there's anyone who hasn't experienced the wayward drip of one glaze flowing toward the earth across the perfect application of the previous glaze.

Tips for Success

Keep bisqueware clean. Lotions, or even the oils from your hands, can create resist spots where glaze adheres unevenly or not at all. Throughout all phases of the glazing process, including loading and unloading the kiln, handle bisqueware with a clean pair of disposable gloves (figure 1). If you think your bisqueware has been compromised—splashed with something, covered with grime, or maybe handled by a visitor—bisque it again rather than risk a crawling glaze.

Remove all dust before glazing including bisque dust, studio dust and even household or street dust. Use an air compressor for foolproof results, but work outside or in a well-ventilated area away from your primary workspace, as bisque dust is extremely abrasive to your lungs (figure 2).

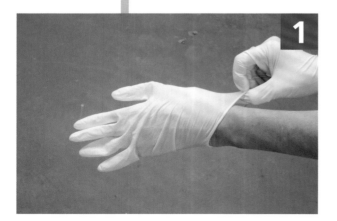

Use silicon carbide paper to remove any rough spots you missed before bisque firing. Place your work on a piece of foam to prevent chipping. After sanding, wipe with a damp sponge to remove all traces of sanding dust (figure 3).

Use a damp sponge instead of rinsing, which should be kept to a minimum. Wring the sponge thoroughly and rotate it so each area is only used once. I tend to use half a dozen or so of those orange round synthetic sponges during any given glazing session (figure 4).

Glazes must be well mixed. I use an electric drill with a Jiffy Mixer attached (figure 5). If there is dry glaze caked on the sides of the bucket, sieve the glaze, then return it to a clean bucket.

Glaze all the interiors of your pots first by pouring the glaze in, then rolling it around for complete coverage. For complex pieces requiring a number of glazing steps, glaze the insides the day before to give you a drier surface to work with, especially for brushing (figure 6).

When removing unwanted glaze, scrape off as much of it as you can with a dental tool or a similar small metal scraper to keep a sharp line. A damp sponge removes the remaining

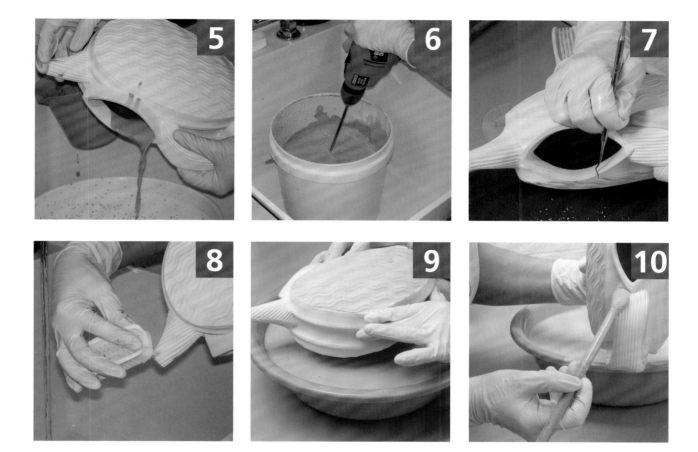

glaze with a few strokes, keeping water usage to a minimum (figure 7).

Use a stiff brush to help clean glaze drips out of texture (figure 8).

For dipping glazes, select an appropriately sized container for the work at hand. I have lots of different sizes of shallow bowls that are perfect for dipping the sides of my pieces. Wide shallow bowls allow me to see what I'm doing, so I even use them for smaller things that fit into the glaze bucket (figure 9).

When you can't dip or pour, it's time for brushing. Watch your bisque as you brush—glaze is shiny and wet when first applied, then becomes matt as the bisque absorbs the water. If you recoat too soon over a damp coat, you'll move the foundation layer rather than imparting a second coat (figure 10).

Consider gravity when brushing and hold the pot both to encourage the glaze to go where you want it to and to keep it from running where you don't want it (figure 11).

If a drip flows onto a previously glazed surface, stop, set the pot down and wait. Resist the urge to wipe the drip with a sponge. Let the drip dry, then carefully scrape it off with a dental tool or metal rib. Use a small compact brush to wipe away glaze in

Brushes

I use sumi brushes, which have long bristles that come to a point, but in the past, I have also used hake and multi-stemmed hake brushes for large areas. Experiment with all the long, springy-bristled brushes. Mop brushes might work for you, but don't buy expensive water-color brushes. Applying glaze is a cruder application than watercolor, and an expensive, fine water-color brush won't work as well for a glaze as a cheap hake from the ceramic supply store.

A brush with long, springy bristles that come to a point is best. Successful brushing not only relies on technique of application, but also the glazes you're using and the temperature you're firing to. Some glazes lend themselves well to brushing, while others are more finicky. Make wide tiles representative of your surfaces and use them to test how well your glazes take to brushing.

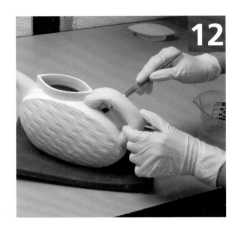

areas you can't reach with a sponge (figure 12).

Don't brush glaze from the big glaze bucket. Pour a small amount into a cup, then briskly stir it occasionally to ensure that it stays properly mixed. Keep a large, damp sponge nearby to keep the brush handle clean. Stray drips often start with a handle full of glaze (figure 13).

If you're glazing pots that don't have a defined foot, push them across a piece of 220-grit silicon carbide sandpaper. The sandpaper removes some of the glaze from the contact areas, indicating where you need to wipe off the remaining glaze.

Volumetric Glazes

by Sumi von Dassow

Test glazes, each consisting of 8 parts Sumi's Volumetric Clear to 1 part Mason stain. Back row, left to right: stain 6319 (Lavender), 6364 (Turquoise) and 6387 (Mulberry). Front row, left to right: stain 6000 (Shell Pink), 6407 (Marigold), 6121 (Saturn Orange) and 6006 (Deep Crimson). Tests are on cones made from slabs rolled out on lace to show how the glaze looks on a textured surface.

People new to glazing may be unsure whether they really want to mix up their own glazes, but they would like to experiment. Since the cost of an accurate gram scale can be an obstacle, an economical way to get started is with a volumetric recipe. Such a recipe requires the ingredients to be measured in cups (or teaspoons, tablespoons or buckets). While less exact than weighing ingredients to the tenth of a gram, this type of recipe can yield fine results and lends itself to experimentation.

A good place to start might be with the very basic recipe of 2 parts colemanite to 1 part Kona F-4 feldspar to 1 part silica. This becomes a clear glaze at cone 5-6, but because of the high level of boron in the colemanite, it's rather milky. It's easy to add various coloring oxides or opacifiers in teaspoons and tablespoons to achieve a wide range of colors from this simple recipe.

Other experiments might be to substitute various feldspars for the Kona F-4, or to try simple additions of other common glaze ingredients. Keeping a supply of test tiles handy—or even pieces of broken bisque-ware—means that any time you get the urge to mix up a quick experimental glaze, you'll have something to try it on.

Learning about glazes this way undoubtedly produces in some strange results, as well as some successful surprises. As long as you keep good records, you'll gradually add to your store of knowledge, and develop familiarity with the many glaze materials in a fun and nonstressful way.

Plate glazed with Sumi's Volumetric Clear Glaze with commercial stain, fired to cone 6 oxidation.

Detail of carved orchid plate with Sumi's Volumetric Clear Glaze mixed with commercial stain fired to cone 6 oxidation.

While such experimentation isn't likely to satisfy any potter forever, it offers an easy way to play with mixing and using glazes at home without requiring a large investment in equipment and materials or a great deal of space. Eventually, a gram scale will probably find its way into your studio, and you'll be on your way to having a collection of 5-gallon buckets and filling the cupboards with raw materials.

Mixing a Glaze

A glaze screen, preferably about 80 mesh, is an essential piece of equipment for straining wet glaze before use. It's helpful to screen the glaze through a 40-mesh screen first to eliminate large lumps. You can purchase screens from pottery supply stores. You can also make one from window screen, though you won't be able to get a fine mesh.

The easiest way to work the glaze through the screen is with your fingers, wearing rubber gloves. It's also very helpful to dry-mix the ingredients, then wait at least a day after adding the water before stirring or screening the mixture.

Volumetric Recipe

The following recipe was developed from the basic recipe given (see sto-

ry), and modified to reduce the milkiness and add the extra calcium required by many commercial stains.

The nice thing about this glaze recipe is that not only is it easy to mix, but with stains you can mix up several different colors of glaze, using only five basic ingredients.

The stains can also be mixed into the clay body or into engobes and painted onto the pot before bisque firing. This glaze can then be applied as a clear base. It can also be applied to a pot and decorated with stains mixed with a little glaze.

Recipes

Sumi's Volumetric Clear Glaze
Cone 6

Colemanite	3 parts
Magnesium Carbonate	2
Whiting	1
Kona F-4 feldspar	5
Silica	3
	14 parts

Add stain in amounts between 1 and 2 parts. The pink and red stains work nicely in a ratio of 8 parts base mix to 1 part stain. To test several colors, mix up a batch using large units such as cups. Mix the dry ingredients together thoroughly by shaking them in a large sealable bag or in a bucket with a tight lid; allow to settle before opening. Use 2 tablespoons of stain to each standard (8-ounce) cup of glaze mix.

A Simple Approach to Glaze Testing

by Jonathan Kaplan

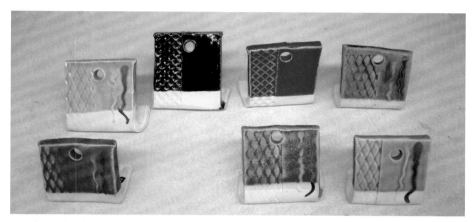

An organized system for testing glazes is simple to implement and can provide a valuable record you'll be able to access for years.

Testing glazes has both educational and practical advantages. A methodical and well-organized regimen can provide you with a great deal of very useful information. You can learn how glazes work alone and in combination with other glazes, engobes and other decorative processes. If a glaze shows potential for problems, you can make adjustments to it or choose to try another glaze. You can learn about the materials, their properties and how they function in a glaze. Here's a simple system that's easy, repeatable and understandable, requiring only a small investment of time and some very basic equipment.

Test Tiles

Test tiles are the heart of the system since a test glaze sits on the tile and provides information on its fired properties. Tiles can be thrown, extruded or made from slabs of your clay body.

If you're testing glazes on different clay bodies, make sure you mark the tiles with a code for that particular body. Test tiles can show a host of additional information if they're prepared correctly, for example:

Angle—bending a section or creating an angled tile provides information about the fluidity of a glaze.

Texture—a textured pattern shows how glazes break "thick and thin" over a surface.

Color—applying white and black engobes on green tile shows how a fired glaze breaks over the raised colored clay.

Hole—a hole in the tile provides a way to display it on a board or secure it to the glaze bucket with a twist tie, wire or string.

In about 2 hours of work in an afternoon, I can easily produce a few hundred test tiles, which is a good amount to have on hand.

Record Keeping

Keep your identification system simple and you'll be able to refer to your notes years after a test. At the base of each tile, use black underglaze to write the date in MMDDYY format, for example, 021307 for February 13, 2007, then add the test number for that day. (Note: Don't write on the bottom of the tile as it can leave a ghost image from the underglaze on the kiln shelf.) Enter these numbers in a glaze notebook next to each test. There's no reason to include any other information on the test tile other than the date and test number as all the other information pertaining to the glaze is in your notebook.

You can also use computer glaze programs as a database for your glazes. There are many excellent applications for PC and Macintosh, such as Insight, Hyperglaze, Matrix and Glaze Master. If using a computer, be sure to always have a hard copy or electronic backup of your work. While I use glaze calculation software to calculate my batch sizes and help with correcting any problems, most entries in my notebook are by longhand.

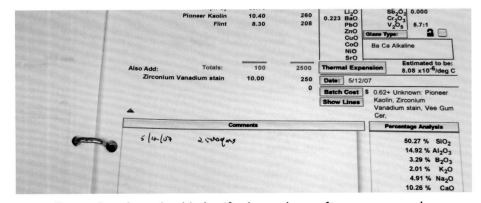

A self-supporting angled tile with texture, as well as black-and-white slip, provides information on several properties of a glaze.

Keep all notes in a three-ring binder. If using a glaze software program, be sure to print out a hard copy for a permanent record.

Example

Granny's Shorts
Cone 4-7

Whiting	14.0 %
Gerstley Borate	42.0
Custer Feldspar	49.0
Plastic Vitrox Clay (PV Clay)	21.0
Silica	14.0
	140.0 %

Divide each amount by 140 to convert to a 100 batch

Whiting	14/140=10
Gerstley Borate	42/140=30
Custer Feldspar	49/140=35
Plastic Vitrox Clay (PV Clay) . .	21/140=15
Silica	14/140=10
	100

Whiting	10×20=200
Gerstley Borate	30×20=600
Custer Feldspar	35×20=700
Plastic Vitrox Clay	15x20=300
Silica	10×20=200
	2000

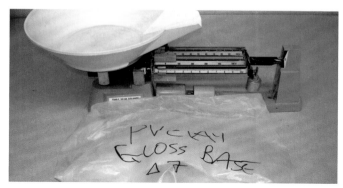

Weigh out materials for a test base glaze into a large resealable plastic bag. Label the bag.

After measuring out a 100 gram test batch, carefully add colorants.

Testing Method

Step 1. Select two glazes. For simple glaze testing, work with only two glazes at one time. This allows you to develop a fairly organized way of working with glazes directed toward what you need to accomplish without getting so overloaded with information that you lose track.

Step 2. Convert the recipes. The batch recipe should add up to 100. If it doesn't, divide the total of the original glaze into the amount of each ingredient. Do not include any colorants or additives in your calculations, just the basic recipe.

Step 3. Calculate the batch. When testing, mix 2000 grams of dry materials to make a gallon of glaze. This is done by simply multiplying each number in the batch formula by 20. For example:

Step 4. Weigh the ingredients. Use a gram scale to measure out the ingredients for the batch glaze. After weighing each ingredient, double check weight on the scale, then place it in a large resealable storage bag.

TIP

You can bend the handle of an old toothbrush by holding it over a heat gun or hair dryer until it's pliable.

As you add each ingredient, check it off the list in the notebook. Since this is base glaze, do not add any colorants or additives.

Step 5. Dry mix the glaze. Seal the bag and mix the ingredients by dumping the materials back and forth to ensure good dispersion. Label the bag with a permanent marker with the name of the glaze, date and cone number.

Step 6. Select test materials. I've found that if I write down all the tests I wish to do prior to any mixing, the testing sequence goes much faster and is better organized. Select metallic colorants (for example, iron oxide, cobalt oxide, copper carbonate) or any pigments (commercial stains) to test. Many books have lists of coloring oxides percentages sorted by temperature and atmosphere that you can use as a reference point.

Step 7. Mix a test. You'll need 100 grams of dry mix for a test which means you'll get 20 tests from a batch. When mixed with 100–125ml of water (3.4–4.2 oz.), a 100 gram test batch yields approximately 1 cup of liquid glaze. Weigh out 100 grams of dry mix, then move then add the additional test material to it. By carefully adding the required amount of coloring material, you can be precise with any addition.

Step 8. Blending. Use an old kitchen drink mixer or blender to mix test batches. (Caution: These mixers must no longer be used for food.) Allow the materials to slake for a few minutes, then blend for a few seconds.

Step 9. Sieve the glaze. Taking a small 100 mesh test sieve and a small clear plastic cup, pour the mixed material through the sieve. Use a bent toothbrush to help the wet material through the sieve. Mark the cup with the date and test number.

Step 10. Glaze a tile. Take a test tile and wipe the surface with a damp sponge to remove any dust. Dip the tile into the glaze and hold it there while slowly counting to 10. The "10 count" allows a sufficient quantity of wet glaze to adhere to the surface. Remove the tile slowly from the cup, allow it to dry then label it with the date and test number. Save the test glaze for a few days in case you need to retest or adjust the mix.

Two Times Better

If you test two base glazes at one time, you can easily add coloring oxides or stains to each base without much extra effort. In addition, you can now put one glaze over another to see how they interact with each other. First, create a series of tiles with glaze #1 over glaze #2, then a set with glaze #2 over glaze #1. You only need to dip a small section of the top of each tile to provide enough glaze to interact with what is below it and not run off the tile.

Spray Those Glazes

by Kathy Chamberlin

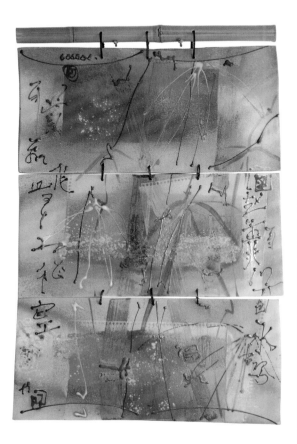

Spraying glaze onto your ware, instead of dipping it or applying it by brush, can be an exciting way to vary your aesthetic results. By overlapping your strokes and planning your coverage, you can achieve aesthetically interesting visual and textural results.

Your success in spraying glazes depends as much on your preparation, your organization and your thoroughness as on your technique itself. Here's how to get the best results.

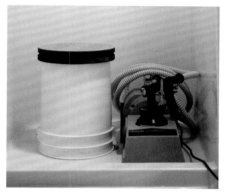

A fiberglass shower stall serves as a spray booth for applying glazes. You'll also need a high-volume, low-pressure spray gun, a banding wheel/turntable, a facemask or respirator, rubber gloves and glazes.

Setting Up the Spray Booth

To get set up, you'll need a spray booth; a spray gun; a banding wheel turntable; protective clothing, mask and eyewear; a five-gallon bucket and, of course, glazes. For me, an old fiberglass shower stall works great as a spray booth. It allows quick access to water, making cleanup easy. Placed upside down in the stall, the bucket comes in handy to elevate your work area. And it rinses easily when you're done and ready for clean-up.

Be sure to protect yourself from inhaling dangerous vapors or splashing glazes in your eyes. In an open

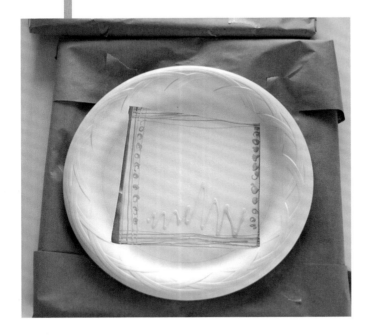

Use cut-outs to get interesting shapes. Here, a square cut out in a round, plastic dinner plate is used to produce a square of glaze.

strain and re-sieve each glaze before use to be sure it's uniform.

To prepare flat surface pieces, use a plate stand or simply hold it upright with your hand or lay it flat on top of the upside-down plastic bucket, and start spraying. To apply glazes to round pieces, you'll need the banding wheel or turntable. Place the banding wheel on top of the bucket and apply the glaze as you slowly turn the pot. Hand turning the banding wheel helps ensure complete glaze coverage and allows you to target specific spots.

Decorating Before Spraying

If you like patterns to show through your glaze, you can decorate your work before glazing. I like to do detail line work with slips on leather-hard ware. You may need to experiment to be sure your lines don't run, and to see which glazes let the designs show through.

I use a lot of slips and underglazes when the ware is leather-hard, and glazes and oxide combinations after the bisque firing. If you plan to use color oxides over the glaze, it's handy to make a sketch of the designs to refer to when you lay out the color. When using oxide combinations, I tend to stay in the iron family, but also use a lot of copper and rutile together.

Also, mastering the pressure and release of brushstrokes, for example, leads to one of my favorite symbols, the bamboo leaf. Plastic squeeze bottles—with or without a metal tip—can be used for trailing slip.

booth, there can be a lot of glaze overspray, so I use a full face and head mask to prevent inhalation and glasses to shield my eyes from splatters or splashes. I always keep a pair of rubber gloves nearby.

Finally, you'll need a high-volume, low-pressure spray gun and a banding wheel/turntable for the actual application of the glaze. Always

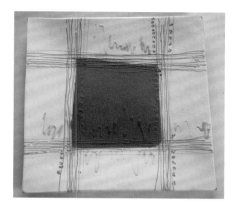

Applying multiple glaze layers with masks creates unique shapes.

Spraying

There are two keys to successful spraying: organization and endurance. The first step is getting organized, and for me that means having enough glaze ready to go so I don't have to stop midway through the application to refill a spray canister. I usually use two spray guns and up to six detachable canisters.

If I plan to use abstract shapes on flat pieces or to mask the inside or outside of baskets so I can glaze them with different colors, I cut these beforehand. The spray gun applies a lot of air pressure, so it may be necessary to tape or hold down the masking material.

The other key is endurance. Once I start, I like to spray all the ware I designate for a particular color before loading a clean canister and moving on to another color. I spray the glaze medium to thick. Since I like to layer a lot of glazes, and seldom pour glazes on clay, each piece has at least two spray applications.

Vertical surfaces like those in baskets also pose a challenge, since many glazes may flow quite differently. If it's hard to reach the bottom of a basket or other vessel, I balance it on a small container like a yogurt cup and spray up under to get good coverage.

When spraying several coats or layers of one glaze, allow each coat to dry before applying the next. I also use masks extensively to create a lot of abstract shapes and stenciling. When spraying baskets, cut outs from plastic plates can mask

Other decorative highlights designed to show through the glaze can enhance your piece.

When spraying a basket, elevate it on a small container so you can spray up from below to ensure good bottom coverage.

the inside or outside, so I can use different glazes that may not interact well if overlapped.

This method of using cut outs to create sharp, clean lines and different overlapping glazes produces deep and beautiful flashing effects.

Glaze Information

I use three different shinos, yellow crystals, white, blue and black barium matts (applied with brushes), and green ash glazes (the best for transparency). I also use three different copper reds, but they are very temperamental. I usually put my green ash glaze under or over the copper red, or use a celadon. The oxides are mostly used in combinations: 1 part iron, 1 part rutile (half-and-half) and some cobalt. Dry wood ash is sprinkled on as surface decoration. I fire my work to cone 10–11 in a reduction atmosphere using a gas fired kiln. The techniques I use can be used with other types of glazes in different temperature ranges.

Clean Up

If you want to prevent problems with residual glaze, dust or glaze build-up on the spray gun, it pays to be obsessive about the cleaning of the spray booth and tools. I rinse out the shower; clean the spray guns with water and rinse each canister; then fill a canister with water and spray out the nozzle until it's rinsed clean.

With an improvised spray booth, a little preparation and a carefully thought-out plan, it's easy to produce interesting new looks on your finished ware with sprayed glazes.

An Approach to Single Firing

by Steven Hill

"Three Ambiguous Bowls," to 8 inches in height, thrown and altered stoneware, ribbed-slip surface, with multiple sprayed glazes, single fired to cone 10 reduction. Hill makes his pieces so they appear as a fluid whole—the undulating rim, the ribbed slip and the cut feet of the bowls work in conjunction with each other.

As I ponder the many years that have passed since I initially wrote about single firing, I think about how much has changed and how much has stayed the same.

In spite of historical precedents, the field of contemporary ceramics has never embraced single firing. In the beginning, I was naïve enough to imagine that studio potters would see the advantages and begin to explore raw glazing. Although I know my article and workshops have inspired many, it has mostly been a solitary road I have traveled. I may not have changed the way the pottery world viewed single firing, but

single firing has perpetually guided and focused my efforts. Through my experiences, I learned to trust the process, to listen to the lessons my materials taught me and to always follow my heart.

Everyone knows that single firing eliminates the bisque, saving both fuel and labor. In reality, however, one must extend the firing during burnout (1400–1700°F), which minimizes fuel savings. The labor saved by not having to stack and unstack bisque firings is indisputable, but this alone would never have been enough. For me, the principle advantage of single firing is the connection I feel to the process.

When I first experienced single firing at a salt glazing workshop taught by Peter Sohngen, I was in undergraduate school and had not yet found my voice in clay. There was often a lag time of weeks waiting for bisqueware and glazing felt like an afterthought, as my heart was always with the new pots spinning off my wheel. Glazing greenware quickly connected the separate stages of pottery making for me; the throwing, decorating and assembly owed naturally into the glazing and firing cycle. The entire process became cohesive.

Single firing has not been without its frustrations, however. My pots have cracked and delaminated in the glazing process. They have blown up and blistered in the firing. I have never felt significant limitations, but raw glazing has always guided me, influencing me to spray glazes, to make robust forms with well-defined rims, and to be more decisive, both when throwing and glazing.

Clay

Until the mid 1990s, I formulated and mixed my own clay bodies, focusing on tight bodies with a high percentage of ball clay. I had considerable success, but was never able to totally avoid the frustrations incurred during glazing.

Since 1995, I have been using Laguna B-Mix exclusively. It is an extremely plastic, light gray (in reduction), porcelaneous body with bentonite. It resists rehydration during glazing more effectively than any clay body I have used. In fact I would say if its working properties, color and temperature range appeal to you, that there is almost no other choice. That said, all clay bodies involve compromise and none have universal appeal. For instance, B-Mix's extreme plasticity requires conscientious joinery to avoid drying cracks.

I have always been a precise thrower, avoiding thin spots that can lead to delamination. Delamination can occur as the water penetrates the wall from both sides after glazing and rehydrates the clay, causing it to expand. If the wall is too thin, the clay can rip apart, leaving a void in the center of the wall with a corresponding bump and sometimes a crack on the surface. Although this looks somewhat like bloating, it occurs during glazing, rather than firing. B-Mix nearly eliminated delamination for me, leading to a greater freedom in my throwing and assembly of pots than ever before!

Since most potters use commercial clay, try your current body and see how it works. The unique properties of your clay body will have a tremendous impact on your success and on whether you perceive single firing as a joyful experience or as a needless hassle. There are literally hundreds of commercial clay bodies available, and a great many of them can be successfully raw glazed and single fired.

Glaze

When raw glazing, one must make the decision whether to glaze bone dry or leather hard. I don't recommend glazing between these stages, as the pot is likely to be dry at the rim and wet near the foot. This will lead to a discrepancy in water absorption and potential cracking. I have always glazed my pots bone dry at the end of a work cycle, but if you glaze leather hard you must glaze when the pot is ready. The pores of leather hard pots are still partially filled with water, so there should be lower water absorption and less chance of delamination or cracking. On the other hand, leather hard pots will continue to shrink, requiring a higher percentage of clay in the glaze and thus limiting glaze choice.

When a raw pot is glazed, the clay rehydrates and subsequently swells. Then as the water evaporates it contracts. If the glaze recipe has no clay, it will lack plasticity and flake off as the pot dries. If the glaze contains some clay, but not enough, it is likely to crawl during the firing.

There are a number of other glaze ingredients that, either through flocculation, deflocculation or excessively small particle size, keep glazes wet excessively long after application. Gerstley borate is a real culprit and, to a lesser extent, most boron frits. Other ingredients to be wary of are soda ash, tin oxide, zinc oxide and possibly titanium dioxide. Any of these can be used successful-

PHOTOS: AL SURRATT

Bowl, 10½ inches in length, thrown and altered stoneware, with ribbed slip, multiple sprayed glazes, single fired to cone 10 in reduction.

ly, but with an increased chance of delamination. My personal solution has been to spray glazes, as water absorption is minimized. Creative thinking will solve just about any problem in ceramics.

Glaze Application

Just about any glazing technique used for bisqueware can be adapted for single firing. Pouring, dipping and brushing are all viable if you consider water absorption and the potential it has to weaken the wall. However, when pouring and dipping, there is a limit to how many coats can be applied, and both the inside and the outside should be glazed in close succession, so they expand and contract simultaneously. Handling pots can be an issue—certainly glaze tongs are out, but picking up a pot by the rim or squeezing the foot also can lead to cracking.

For the last ten years spraying has been my primary glazing technique. I pour the interior of all enclosed forms, but use the spray gun to glaze the exterior of pots, and for both the inside and outside surfaces of open forms. The undeniable advantage of spraying is that water evaporates as the glaze travels from the tip of the spray gun to the clay surface. Multiple layers can be applied without the risk of excess water absorption, making it unnecessary to glaze the outside of the pot immediately after the interior.

My first experiment with spraying glazes was with a manually operated "flit" gun (made for applying weed killer) in the mid '70s. By the late '70s I was using a small continuously running compressor that was nearly as irritating as a small dog barking at my feet. Eventually I acquired a compressor with a 30-gallon tank and located it in the next room to keep the noise down. I use anywhere from 20–80 pounds of pressure, depending on the gun I'm using and the thickness of the glaze I'm applying. Since the gun is never in constant use, the capacity (in cubic feet per minute (CFM)) of the compressor is not too important. Most portable compressors with an air tank are quite adequate.

My favorite type of spray gun is an automotive siphon-feed touch-up gun with a top-mounted trigger. This type of action is similar to holding a pencil or a brush and I have better control of detail than with a full-sized gun. For most applications, this is a good compromise between the fine control and small capacity of an airbrush and the large capacity, broad coverage and corresponding weight of a full-size spray gun. I have also experimented with HVLP (high-volume, low-pressure) spray guns. They are more efficient, creating less overspray and therefore reducing the amount of glaze fog in the air. Although they are more environmentally friendly, they do not have as fine of control and must be used with a pressurized cup.

Although most of my experience has been using guns with cups attached, there are some real advantages to a remote pressurized paint pot. Over time, using a heavy spray gun contributed to a case of tendonitis in my elbow. Locating the glaze container on the floor takes away most of the weight and thus relieves stress on the arm. These remote pressurized pots are large capacity (2 quarts to 5 gallons) and potentially give better control of the spray pattern and volume of glaze applied. Changing colors is much more time consuming, however. If money weren't a factor, I'd have 15 remote pots set up, each with its own dedicated glaze!

The biggest problem with all automotive spray guns is wear. Due to the abrasive nature of glazes, the fluid tip and needle wear down over time and need to be replaced. Using a spray gun specially made for ceramic glazes, such as the "Critter," can minimize this costly maintenance. These guns operate by a simple atomizer principle and have no inter-

"Melon Pitcher, 14 inches in height, thrown stoneware, with ribbed-slip surface, multiple sprayed glazes, single fired to cone 10 in reduction.

Inset: Doorway of a stucco barn at a working farm named Montestigliano in Tuscany. "Peeling paint is disgraceful in America, but soulful in Italy," says Hill. "I saw the architectural features of my pottery for the first time when I was in Italy, seeing how the rims, handles and feet related to the body of my forms."

nal parts to be worn down by the abrasive action of glazes. Although ideal for classroom situations where they are routinely abused, this type of gun typically provides a coarser spray without the fine adjustment potential of an automotive gun.

In the '70s I sprayed glazes to emulate atmospheric firing. I soon realized the practical advantages and spraying became a primary method. As I became more skilled I developed techniques that allowed me to both isolate color on my rims and feet and subtly blend glazes throughout the body. Now many years later, it is clear how my technical skill and aesthetic sensibility developed side by side, each influencing the other.

Firing

The worst possible disaster when single firing is to blow up pots. All raw pots have water in them (both atmospheric and chemically combined) and unless they were glazed weeks ago, absorbed water. If the temperature rises too quickly as water is turning to steam, an explosion can occur. The tighter the clay body and the thicker the piece, the more likely this is to be a problem. If a pot blows up in a glaze firing, there will be shards scattered throughout the kiln landing on horizontal surfaces such as rims, lids, plates and bowls. I've lost nearly half a kiln load from one explosion!

It's not difficult to safely preheat the kiln, but it does require patience. In fuel burning kilns, the top third of the kiln can be several hundred degrees hotter than the bottom during the early stages of preheating. In a downdraft kiln the bottom will quickly catch up as the chimney begins to draw. Therefore, I recommend a slow preheat to 500°F. I take seven hours, but if you are firing large, thick sculpture you might need to go slower.

Once beyond preheating, the temperature can proceed quickly to the burnout phase. Between 1400–1700°F, the kiln should be oxidizing with enough time allowed for the organic material to thoroughly burn out. Typically, pots go through this temperature range three times: once as the bisque kiln is fired; again as it cools; and a third time during the glaze firing. When single firing you have only one chance to burn out the volatiles! If the atmosphere is not oxidizing or if you go through this stage too fast you risk trapping organic material under the melting glaze. After the glaze melts, the organic vapors begin to escape, causing the glaze to blister, pinhole and, in extreme cases, the clay will bloat.

I fire a Geil gas kiln with a programmable computer. This has been a blessing, as it prevents my impatience from getting in the way of the ideal firing. If I didn't have a computerized kiln I would likely be less careful with preheating and burnout. There is simply no substitute for experimentation with firing schedules to see how they interact with specific clays and glazes.

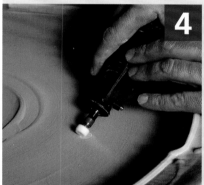

Spraying a Glaze

A large flat pot, such as a platter, gets sprayed on both the front and the back. The back is kept fairly simple; a mat black glaze with an iron saturate sprayed around the edge of the rim. The body is sprayed with a strontium mat, emphasizing the slip spiral applied with a brush while throwing. A transparent oribe green is sprayed to emphasize the spiral movement (figure 1). An iron saturate is sprayed over the strontium mat to turn it into a Tuscan orange (figure 2). The wide rim is sprayed with two iron saturates and a mat black glaze to frame and contrast with the interior of the platter (figure 3). Sometimes, to add a spot of color, I'll take a Dremel tool with a buffing wheel to clean spots on the recently glazed pot (figure 4) and then touch a spot of complementary glaze to fill in the bare spot for contrast (figure 5).

Platter, 21 inches in diameter, thrown and altered stoneware, brushed slip spiral, multiple sprayed glazes, single-fired gas-reduction.

Two mugs, each 5 inches in height, thrown and altered stoneware, trailed slip, with multiple sprayed glazes, single fired to cone 10 in reduction, by Steven Hill.

Firing Schedule (Pre-Reduction)

- Room temperature to 225°F: 3-hour ramp, with a 2-hour soak at 225°F.

- 225–500°F: 2-hour ramp with no soak.

- 500–1500°F: 3-hour ramp, with a 2-hour soak at 1500°F.

- 1500–1700°F: 2-hour ramp, with a 2-hour soak at 1700°F.

- 1700–1800°F: approximately 1 hour in heavy reduction.

- 1800°F–Cone 9: approximately 6 hours in light reduction.

- Cone 9–Cone 10: approximately 1 hour in oxidation. Fired manually once the kiln is in reduction .

Oxidation and soaking are still important if you are single firing in an electric kiln. If you don't vent the kiln by actually drawing fresh air through the kiln chamber, there can be local reduction caused by the carbonaceous material in the clay. This reduction can prevent thorough burnout and cause blistering. Don't just assume you are in oxidation, even if you are firing electrically!

Further In

It is easy to look back and see the profound effect that single firing has had on my work. Although I never saw it as a limitation, the growth of my work has been subtly directed by the constraints of raw glazing. It led to expanded use of the spray gun, which allowed me to both isolate and blend glazes in ways that eventually became a signature.

Obviously, single firing is not for everyone and no one should pursue a way of working that feels uncomfortable. Also, if the goal is extreme delicacy and thinness, deep carving, or complex painterly surface design, there are important reasons to bisque fire. The issue is to follow your passion, whatever it might be, with everything you've got!

With my first single firing experience, I was affected on a primal level and inspired to go further in. As I achieved the necessary skill to focus beyond technique, my artistic vision developed and single firing began to soulfully connect me to my work. I simply opened my eyes and heart, and let influences flow through me. Music, nature, architecture and pottery all left their mark. Single firing helped unify varied sources of inspiration, while determination has given structure to my journey over the years.